I0749345

HELGUERA'S

ARTOONS

ARTOONS

By Pablo Helguera

Jorge Pinto Books Inc.
New York

Artoons
by Pablo Helguera

Published by Jorge Pinto Books Inc., website: www.pintobooks.com

Book design by Charles King, website: www.ckmm.com

ISBN: 978-1-934978-10-8
1-934978-10-8

FOREWORD

Cabaret in nineteen-thirties Berlin. Political jokes whispered in smoky bars in communist Russia. Late-night television in Dick Cheney's America. The truth always bubbles up somehow. Humor thrives whenever and wherever the obvious cannot be said.

And so it is in the world of contemporary art. The art world is hardly a totalitarian state; it actually prides itself on harboring outré personalities and far-out ideas. Even so, as anyone who has been to a gallery opening or a museum gala knows, the art crowd can be comically thin-skinned when confronted with genuine outspokenness. Even Andy Warhol had to be careful about crossing the line. In the company of art dealers and collectors, some things are best left unspoken. Need proof? Try asking, "Why is this picture worth $5 million?" or "Why is the woman in that painting upside down?" and see what happens.

A newcomer to this rarified environment has to master its arcane codes and symbolic landmines. Candor can be risky. The punishment won't be a knock at the door, but it could jeopardize a few dinner-party invitations. To keep out the riff-raff, the language of the art scene is famously cryptic, larded with jargon and Orwellian doublespeak of a pretentious albeit comparably benign variety. Choices of vacation destinations, footwear, or holiday stationery can attain monumental significance. An ever-present fear of being found out-of the-loop, or worse, a philistine, puts art people permanently on edge.

Lucky for us, we have Pablo Helguera to shine a light through the fog. An artist, museum educator, and man about town (specifically, New York City), Helguera is an amateur anthropologist of the art world. He shared his early research in a pithy volume entitled *Manual of Contemporary Art Style*, which doubles as an etiquette manual for aspiring art professionals. With a keen eye and a sharp wit, he set forth the "implicit rules that regulate this milieu," such as: *Good directors are known for their ability to disguise their censorship process. . . . Artists should dress keeping up with fashion, adding an unexpected element (for example, colored socks). . . . The best kind of PR is the one not acknowledged as such.* And so on. It's one of the funniest art books ever written.

Not long ago, Helguera had a kind of Duchampian moment. As well known, Duchamp in his later years pretended to devote himself entirely to the game of chess. In fact, he was working on his final masterpiece, *Étant Donnés*, the famous diorama sculpture now exhibited at the Philadelphia Museum of Art. And likewise, while we all thought Helguera was up to nothing but art making and museum educating, it turned he was working on a special project. The results of this work are contained on the pages of this book.

"I started my artistic life, like most other artists, as a kid drawing cartoons," Helguera has said. He was especially impressed with a book of cartoons from the *New Yorker* by Saul Steinberg, which he found in his grandfather's library while he was growing up in Mexico City. Steinberg became an idol, as did Quino, the Argentinean cartoonist. Cartooning was an important outlet for political expression in Mexico in the nineteen-seventies. Big-name artists like Damian Ortega contributed cartoons to newspapers and magazines. By age eleven–twelve, Helguera was publishing his own. But when it came time to go to college, he decided to be a "serious" artist and stopped making cartoons, other than for friends. Last year was a turning point. Helguera was talking with his museum colleagues about "a rather pedantic artist." He decided to draw the artist, and soon enough, copies of the cartoon were pinned up all around their offices. He had stumbled upon "an escape valve that needed to be tapped," he realized.

For Helguera, drawing cartoons "mainly has to do with my desire to comment on the various idiosyncrasies and absurdities about the art world." The cartoons really do capture the foibles, ironies, and occasional stupidity of the art world with a clarity and economy that only a simple pen drawing and a short piece of text can achieve. They fill an important gap. Cartooning is rarely done in the art world. Honoré Daumier and the journalist Anthony Haden-Guest are among the rare exceptions. Helguera's cartoons are meant to be "by and for the art world." Their point, in his words, is to "make fun not only of ourselves, but also of the way the mainstream looks at contemporary art."

Full disclosure: I had a small hand in all this. In the summer of 2008, Helguera, who contributes occasionally to *artworldsalon*, a website that I co-founded, proposed that we launch a regular cartoon feature. Our editors embraced the idea. I suggested calling the series *Artoons*. For better or for worse, the name stuck. The series continues.

"I think the art world has a really complicated problem with humor," Helguera recently told me. Maybe the problem isn't the humor, but the truth. It may take years of sleuthing for Helguera, the anthropologist, to figure out why this is so. In the meantime, Pablo's *Artoons* can do the talking for us.

András Szántó, October 2008

HELGUERA'S

ARTOONS

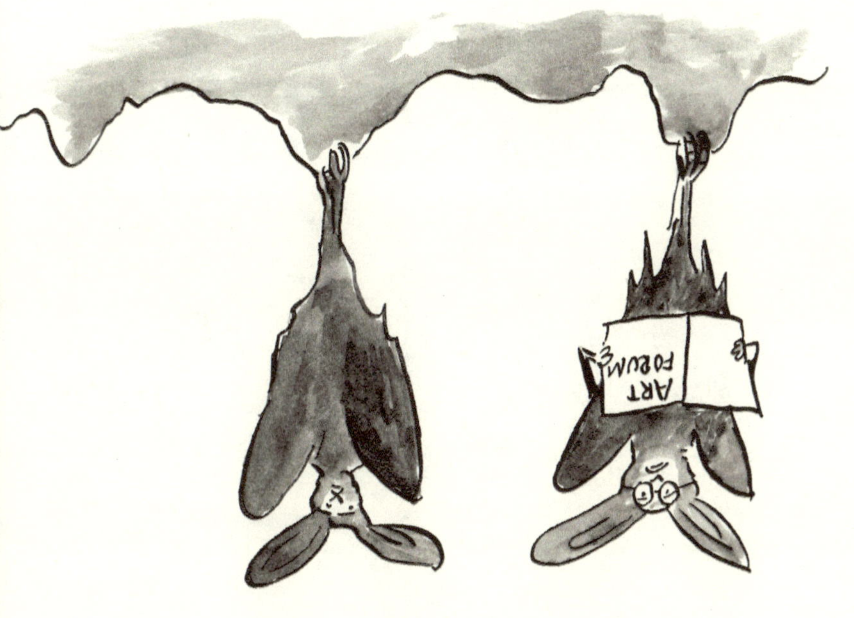

"I don't know about these hot new painters . . . we should just stick with Baselitz."

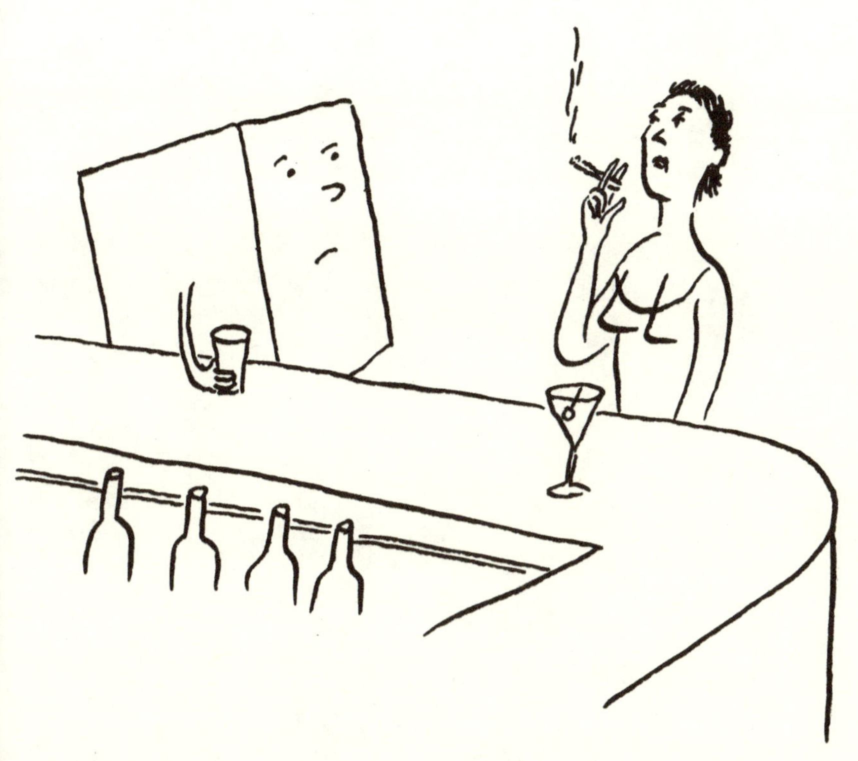

"I am a land artist. I don't do white cubes."

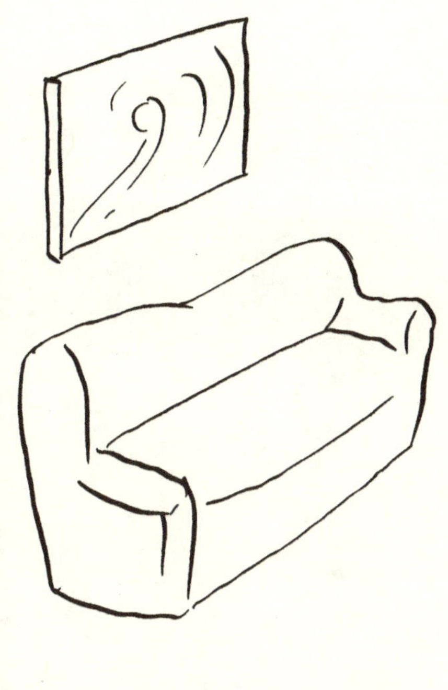
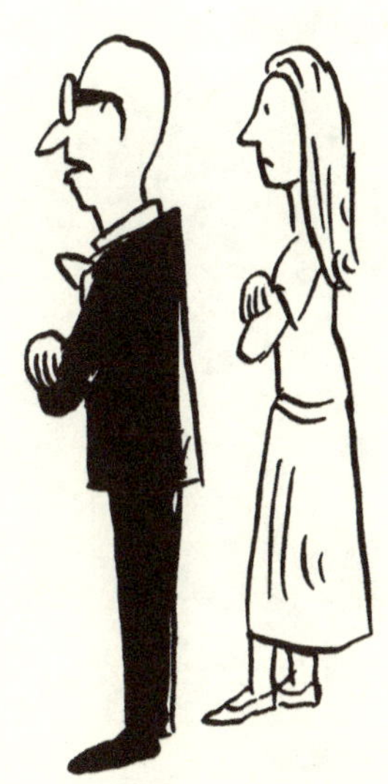

"The theory doesn't match the couch."

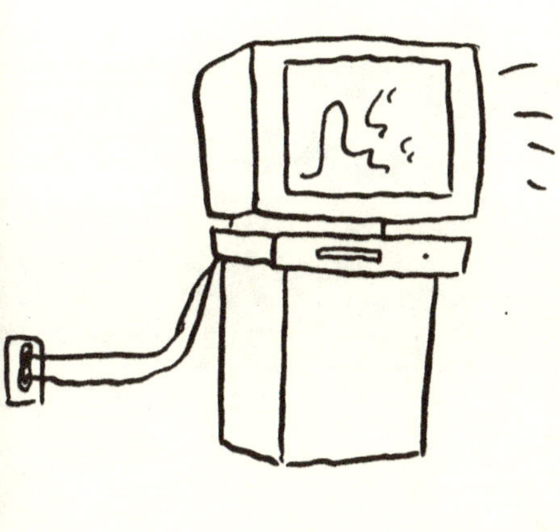
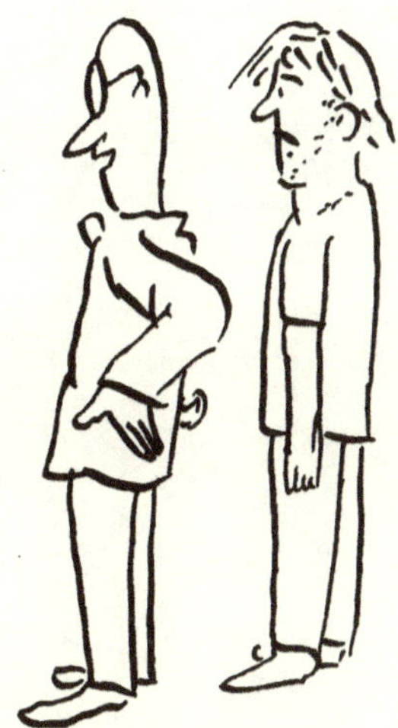

"Could you make an American version without all the Godard references?"

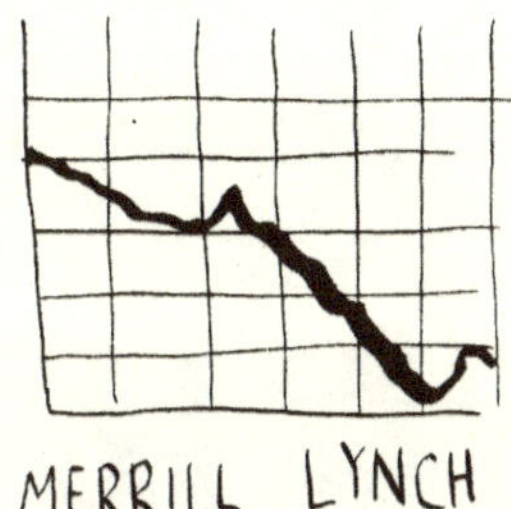

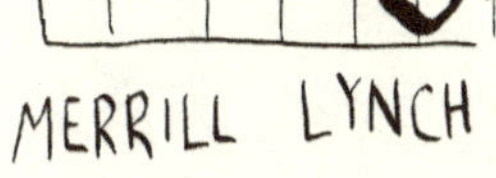

BEAR STEARNS

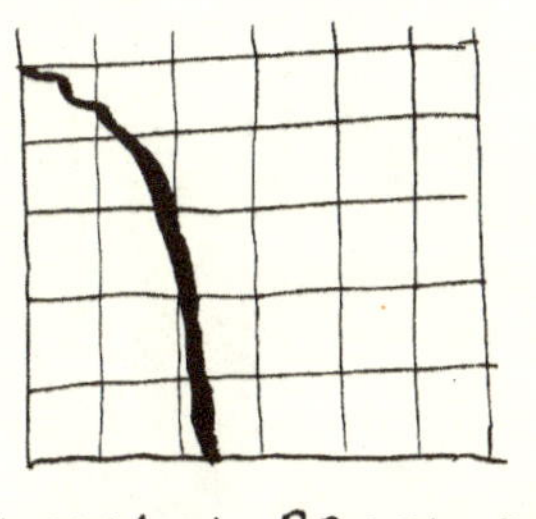

LEHMAN BROTHERS

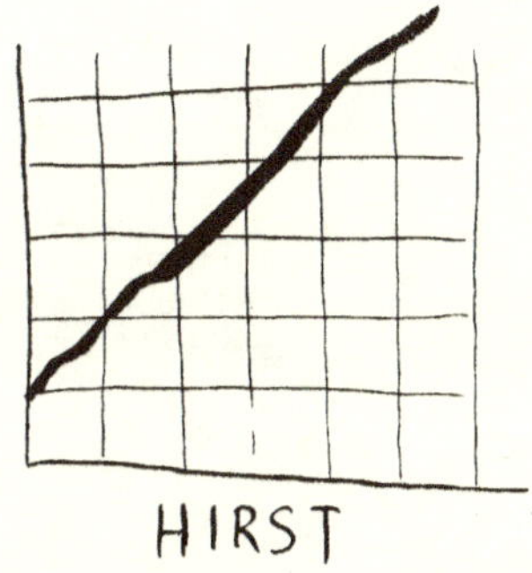

HIRST

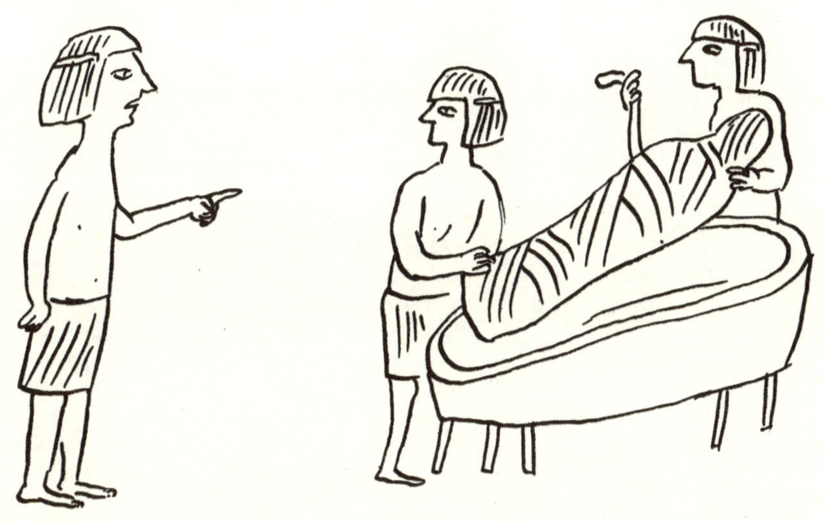

*"Make sure you wrap it extra well.
We don't have insurance for the shipping."*

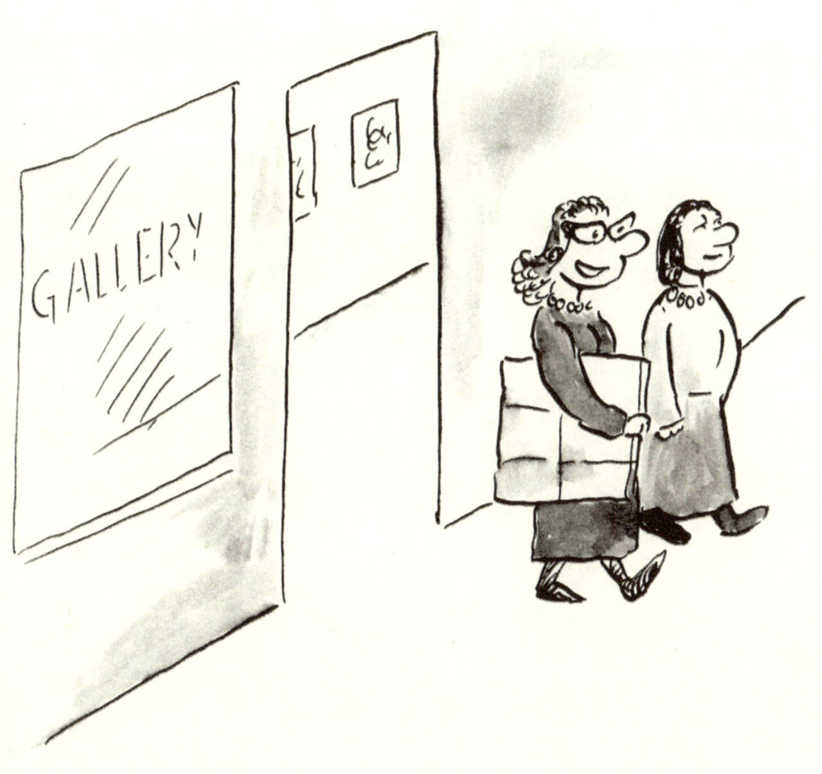

"First I thought that the piece was just awful,
but then I looked at the price."

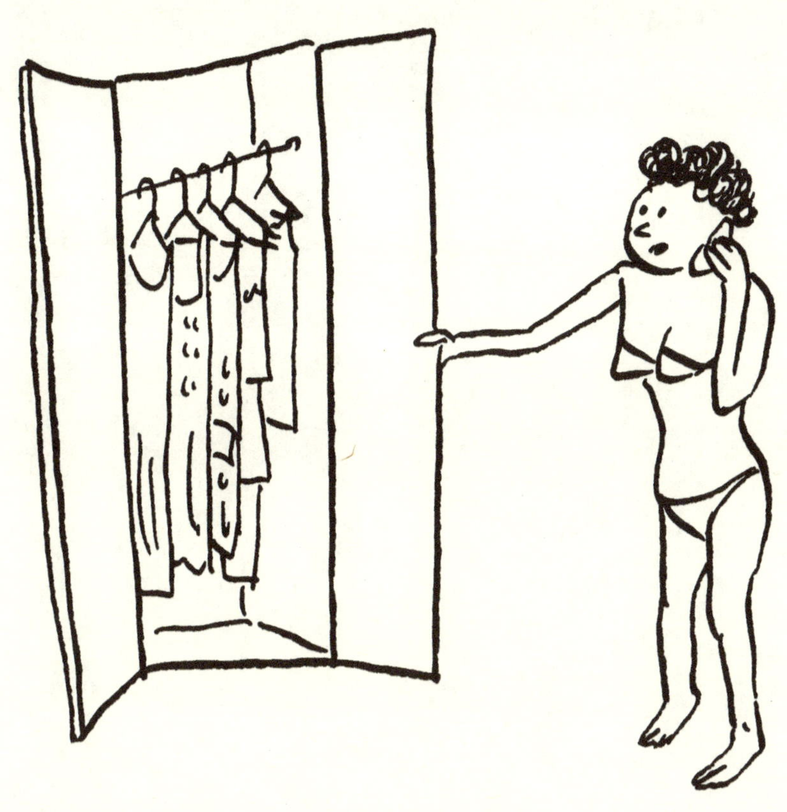

"For the opening I need to wear something that makes me look successful but still in need of a gallery."

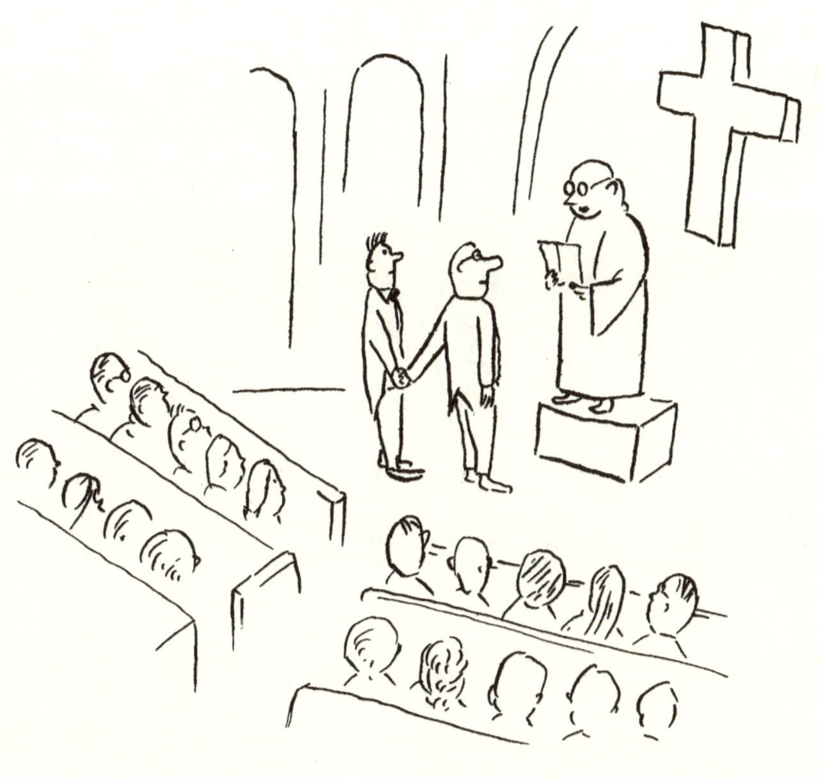

"Matthew, do you take Robert as your dealer 'til death do you part or a more suitable gallery offer comes by?"

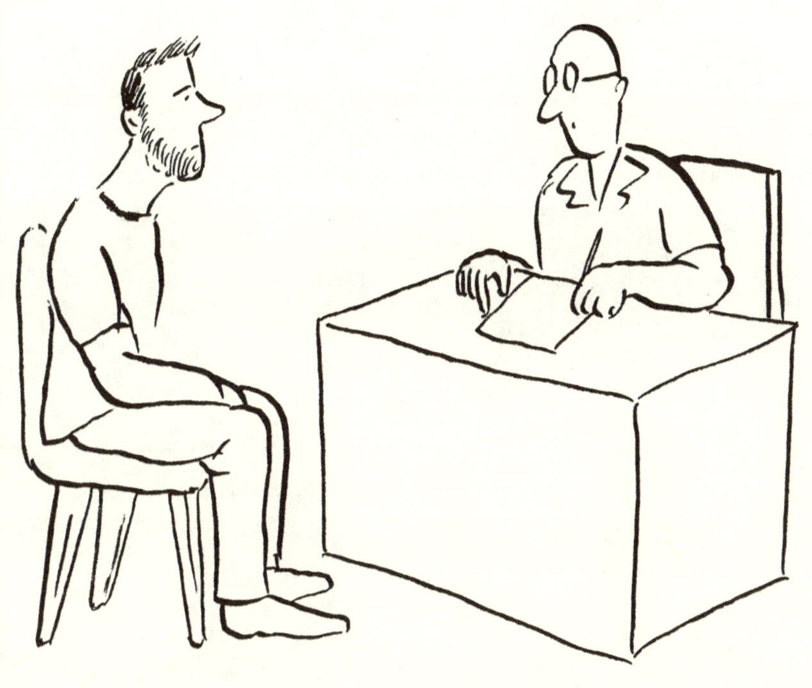

"Have you ever been involved with a terrorist organization, or have you ever made a project for Creative Time?"

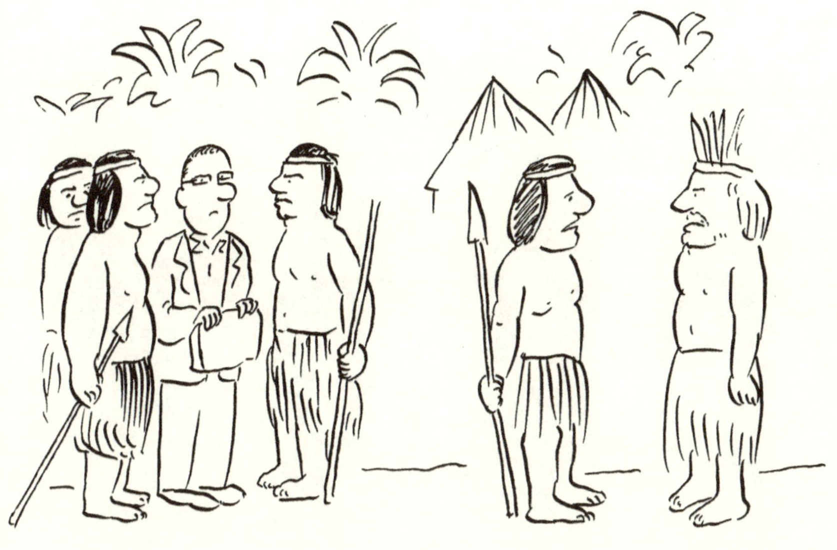

"He says he is curating a biennial and wants to know if anyone here does video."

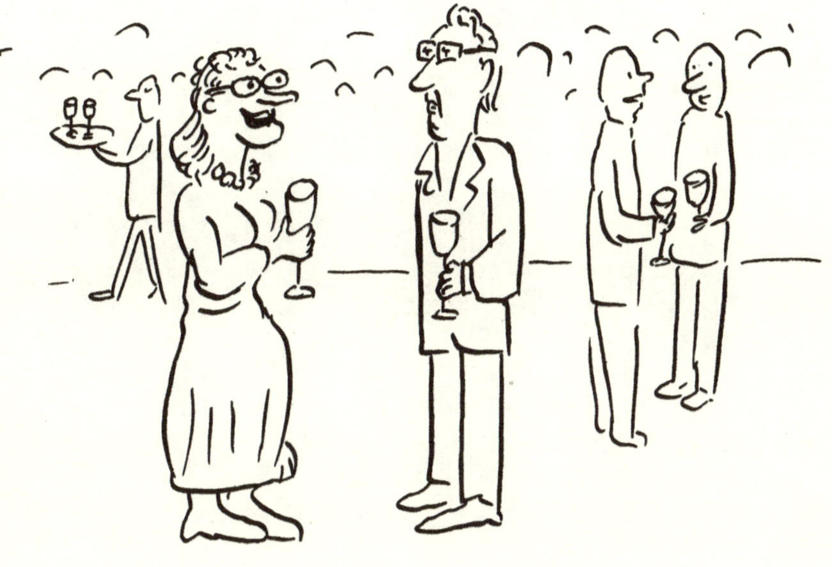

"I always thought you were a fictional character from the art history books."

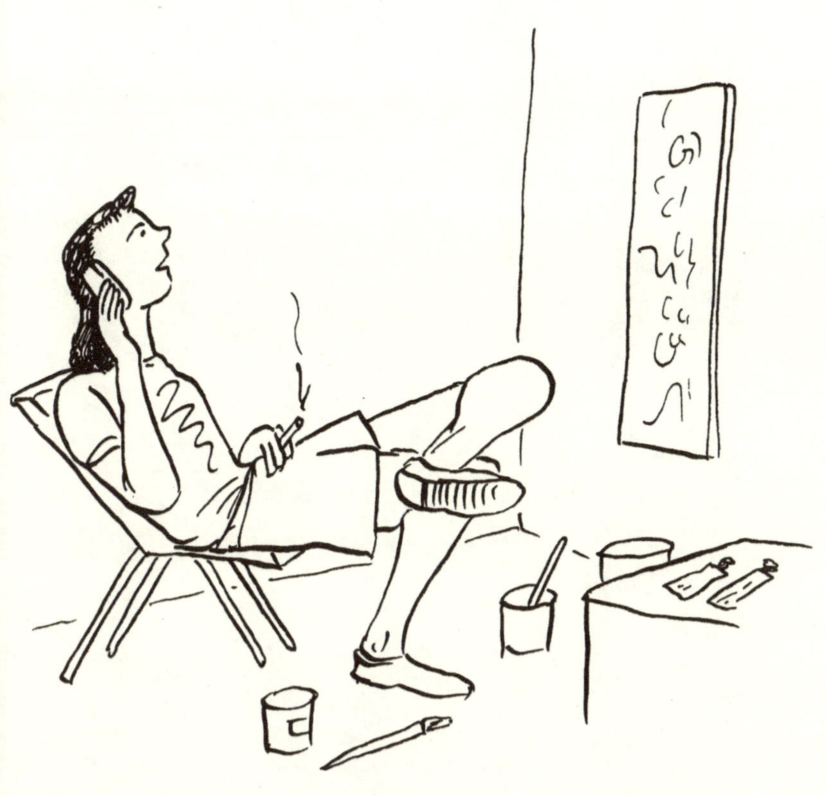

"I'll call you later. My painting is talking to me."

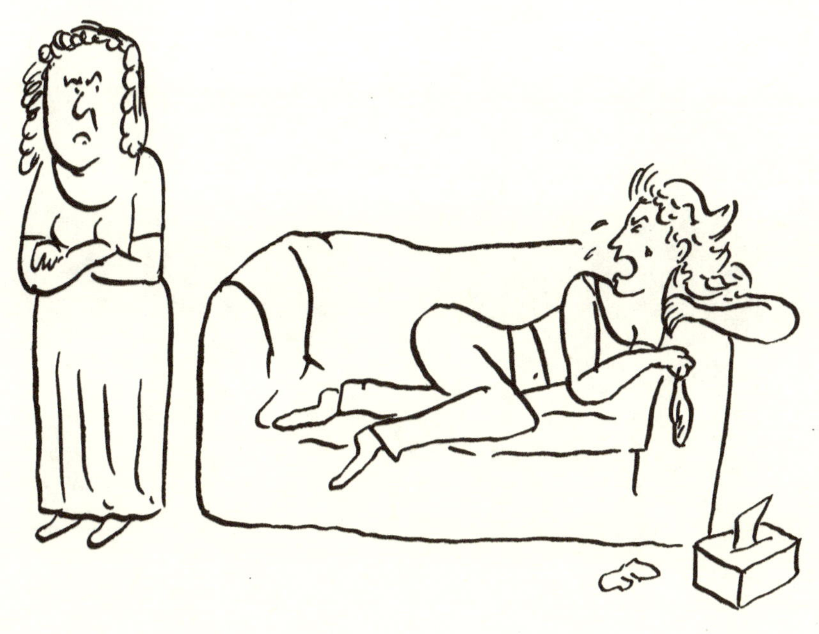

"I don't care that he is an artist from the 80s—
I am in love with him!"

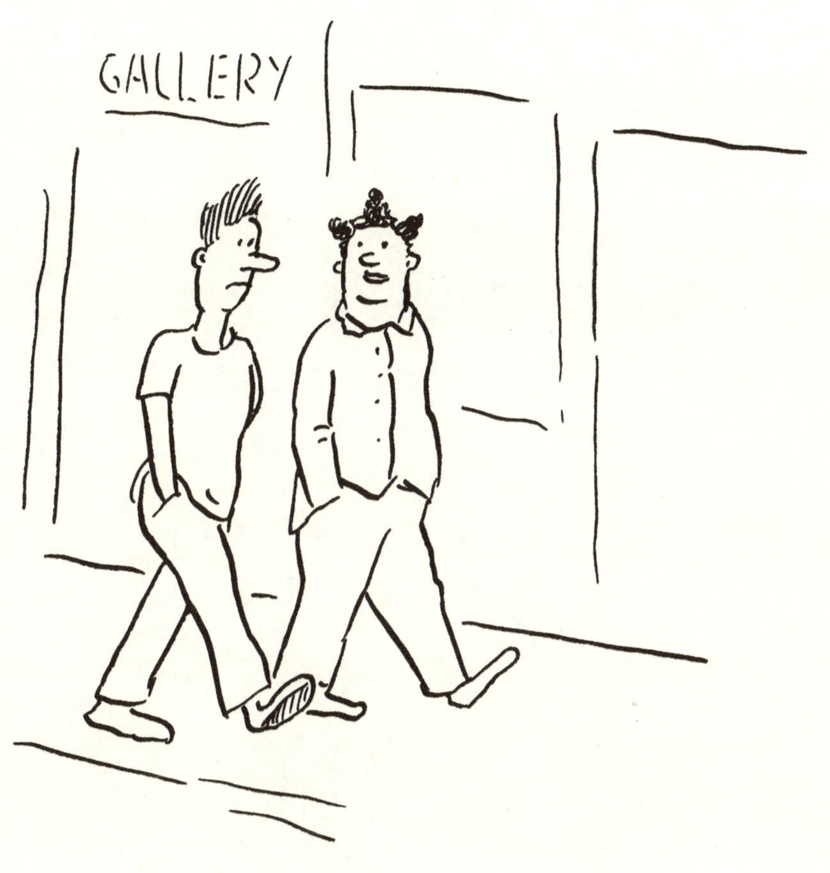

"I just get a lot of shows because I am easy to Google."

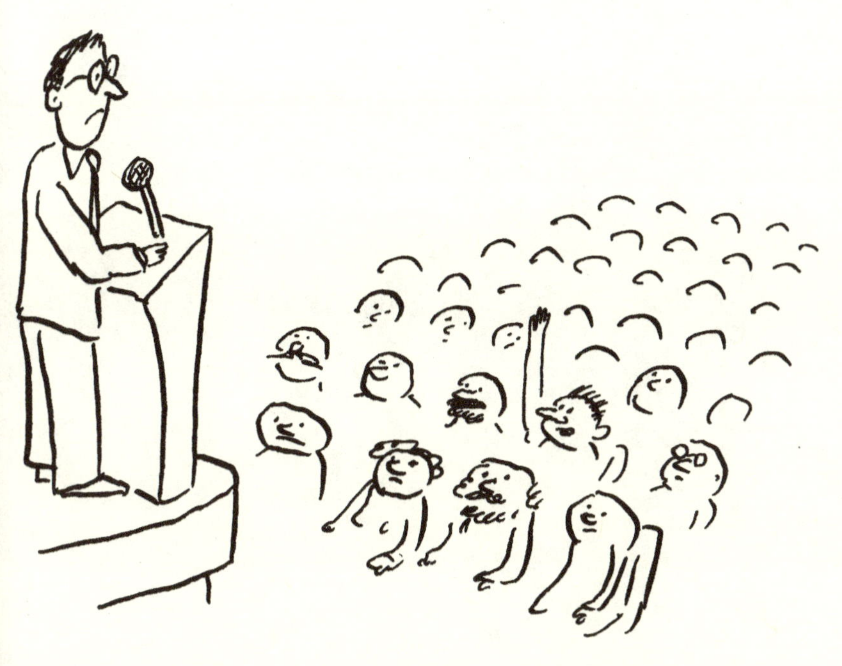

"It's not a question—I just want you and the audience to acknowledge that I exist."

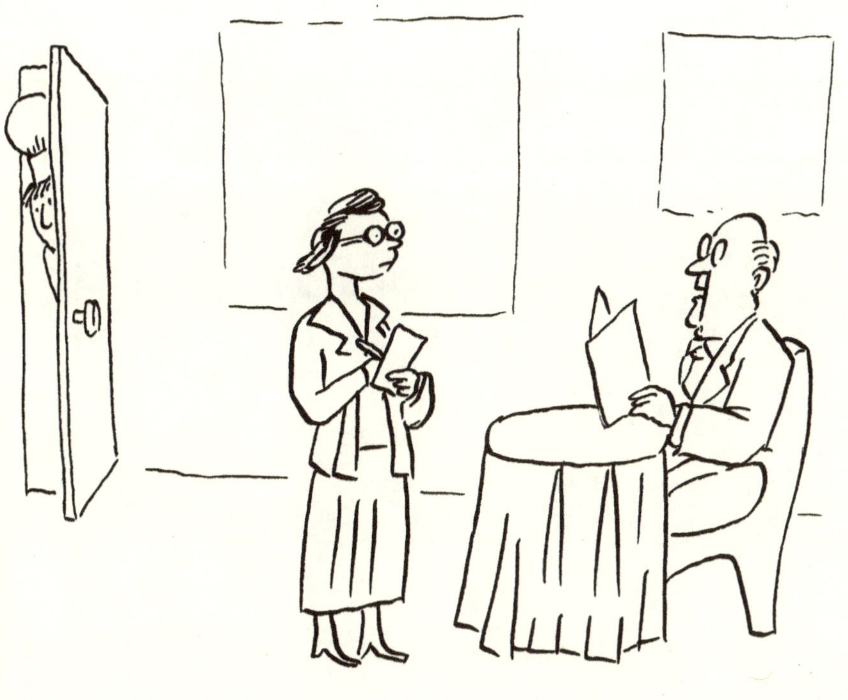

"I will have the post-minimalist installation with a relational twist, but tell the artist not to overdo it like the last time."

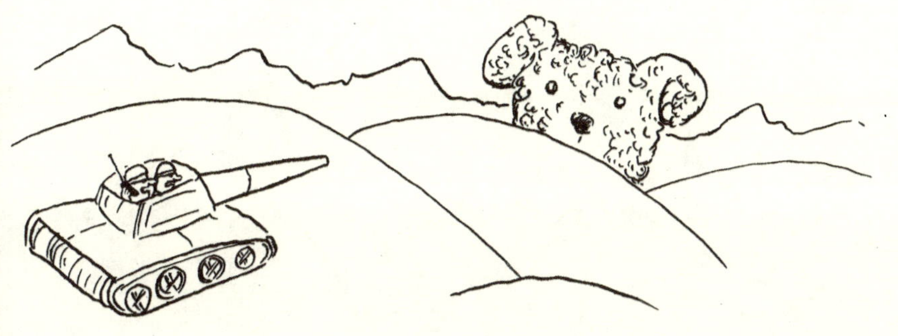

"Alert! The enemy is deploying its Jeff Koons puppy!"

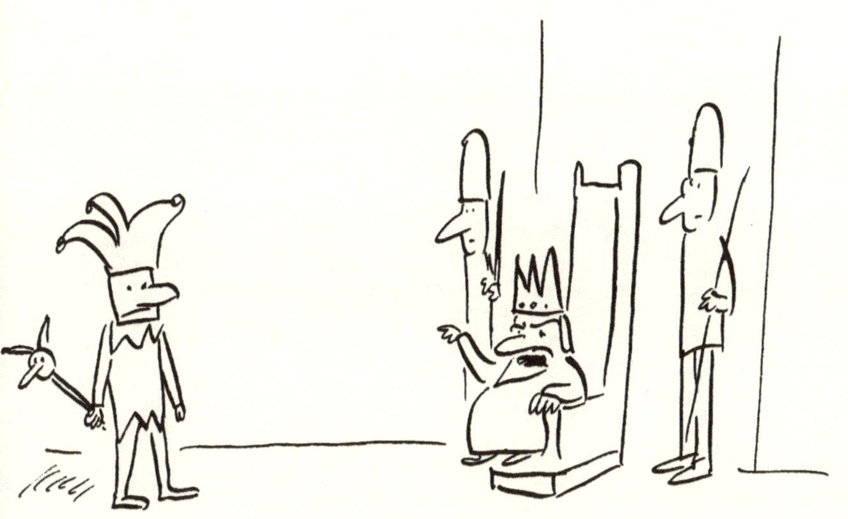

"Jester, I am bored. Make me a Cattelan piece."

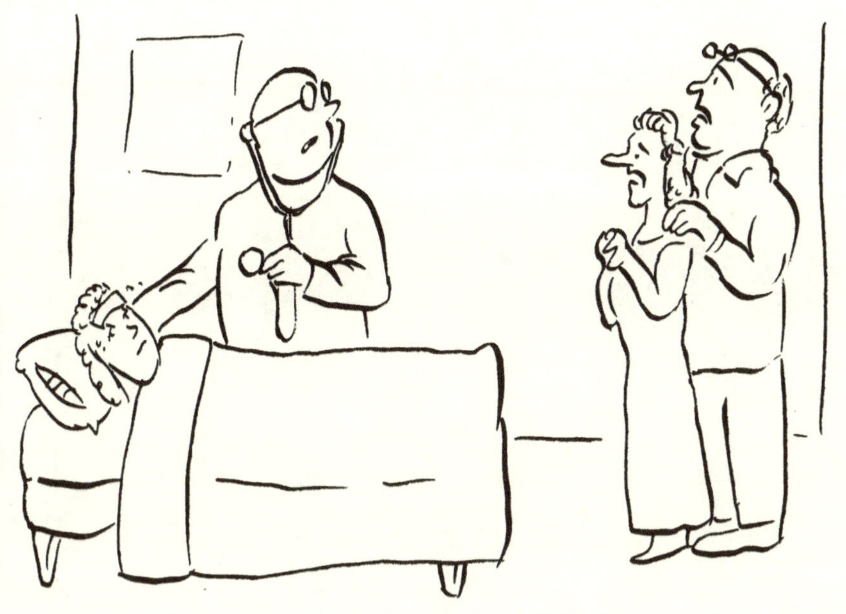

"She's got John Currin Syndrome."

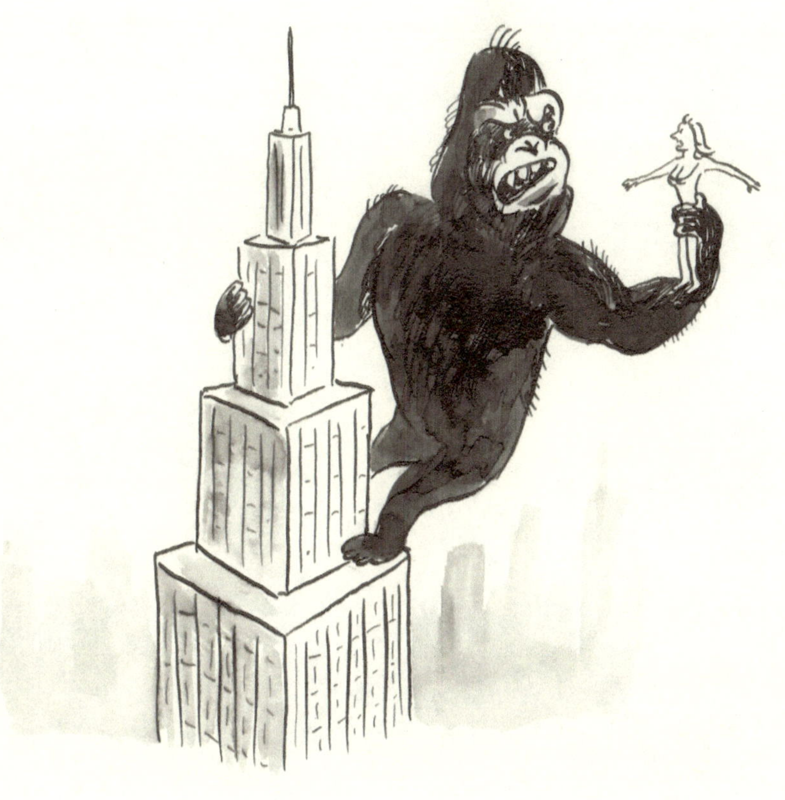

"So the arrangement is this: 60% for me on every sale, and every work you make goes through my gallery."

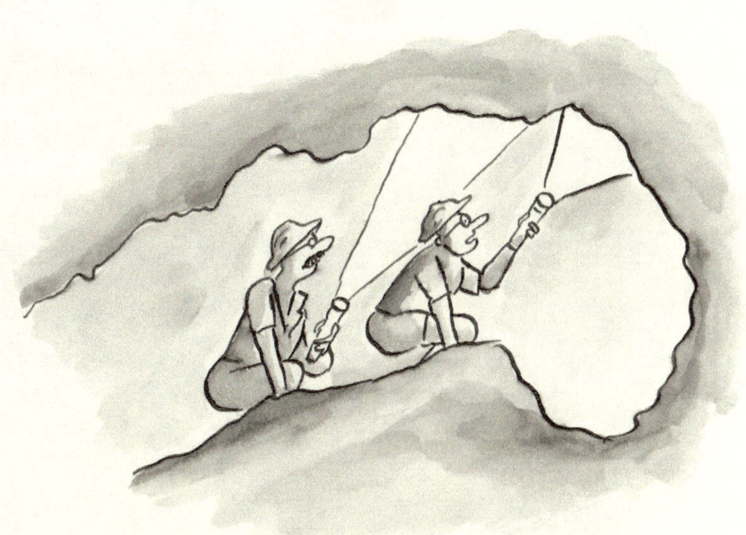

"Looks like Vik Muñiz had a show here."

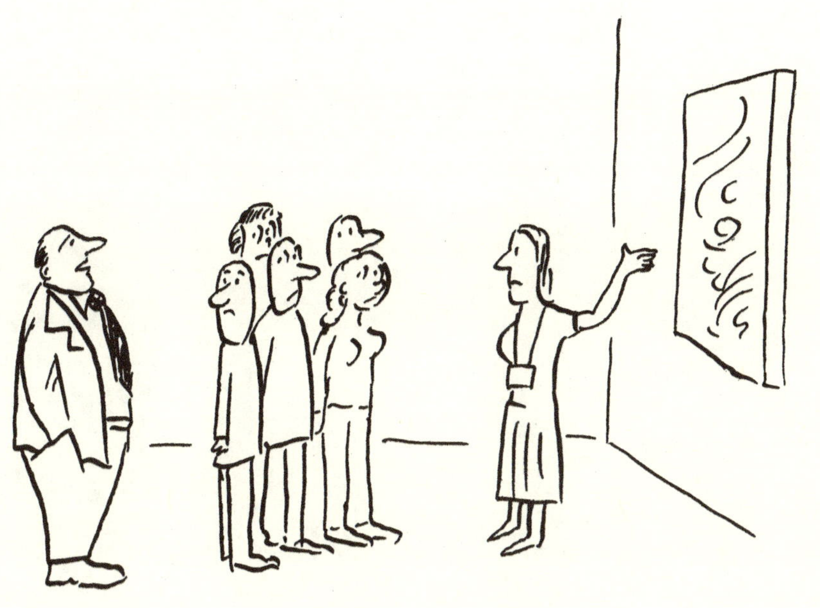

"My corporation could do that."

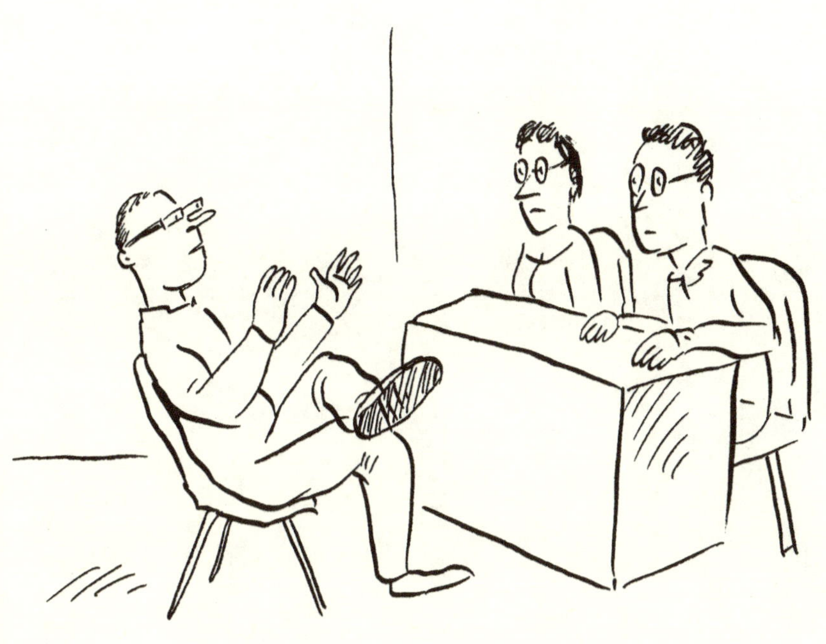

"So my proposal is this: I try to bomb the museum, you try to stop me, and I go down art history as the visionary artist and you as the retrograde curators."

~MUSEUM NAMING OPPORTUNITIES~

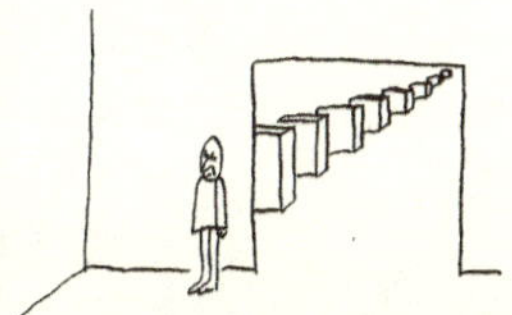

THE JACK M. ZIMMERMAN WING OF DAMIEN HIRST SURPLUS WORKS

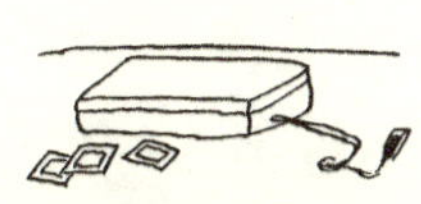

THE BLANCHE KROPP HONORARY 1989 SCANNER

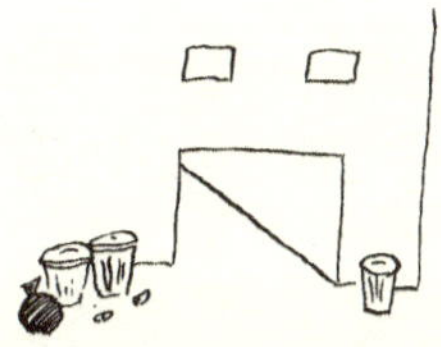

THE ROSAMUND K. J. B REAR-SMITH LOADING DOCK

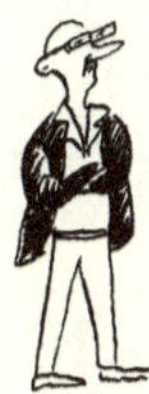

THE RUPERTINA S. WHITE-NIPPLE AUTHORITATIVE CHAIR OF CONTEMPORARY ART

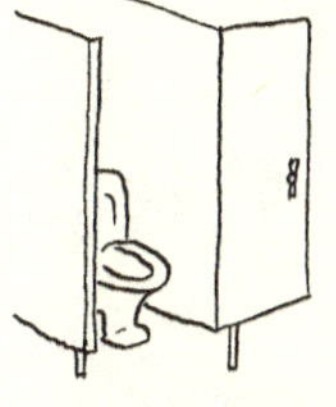

THE LARRY CRAIG MEMORIAL TOILET

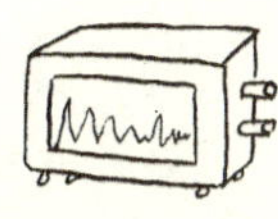

THE BABALÚ F. MUSSOLINI ENDOWED CLIMATE CONTROL WHATEVER MYSTERIOUS THING

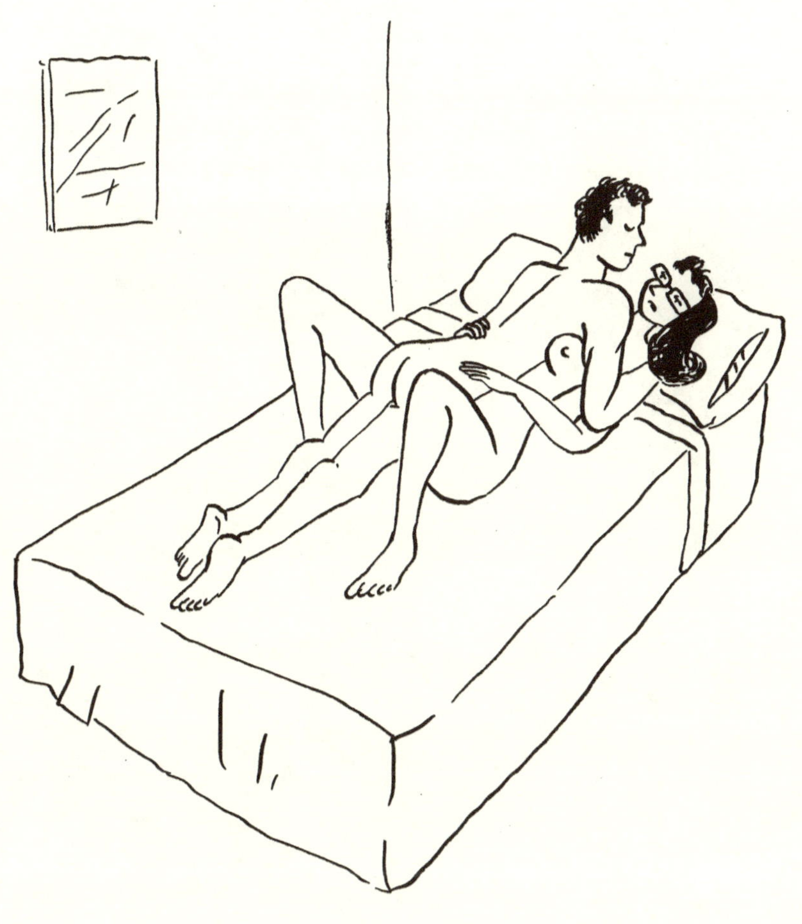

"Now I think I am getting a much better sense of your work."

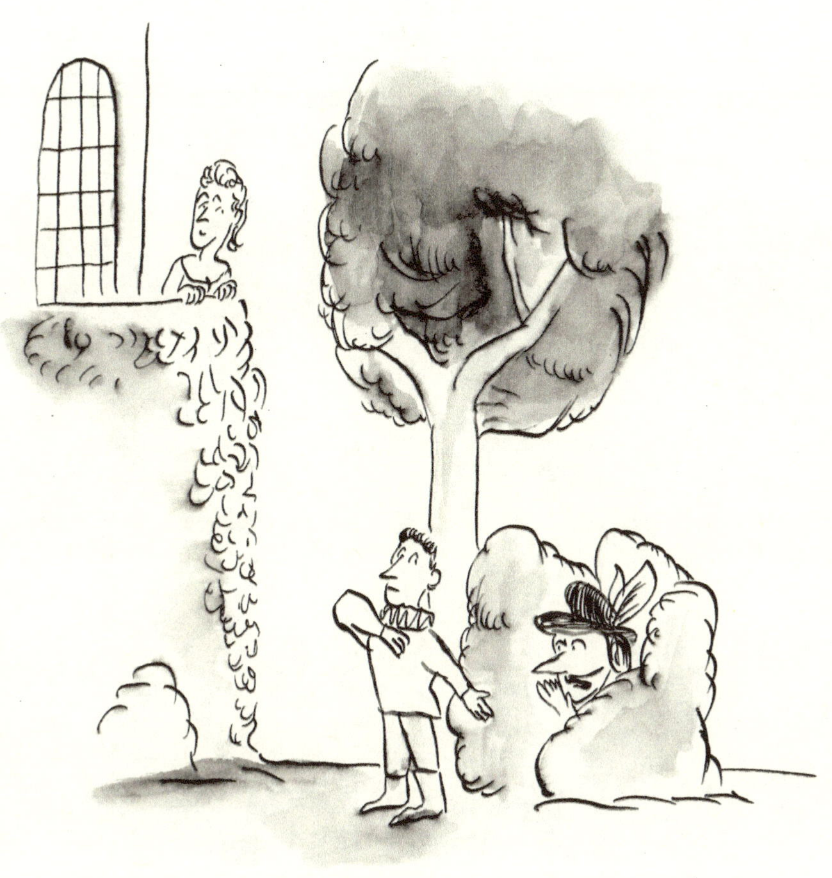

"OK, now tell her that her work is hotter than Rachel Harrison's."

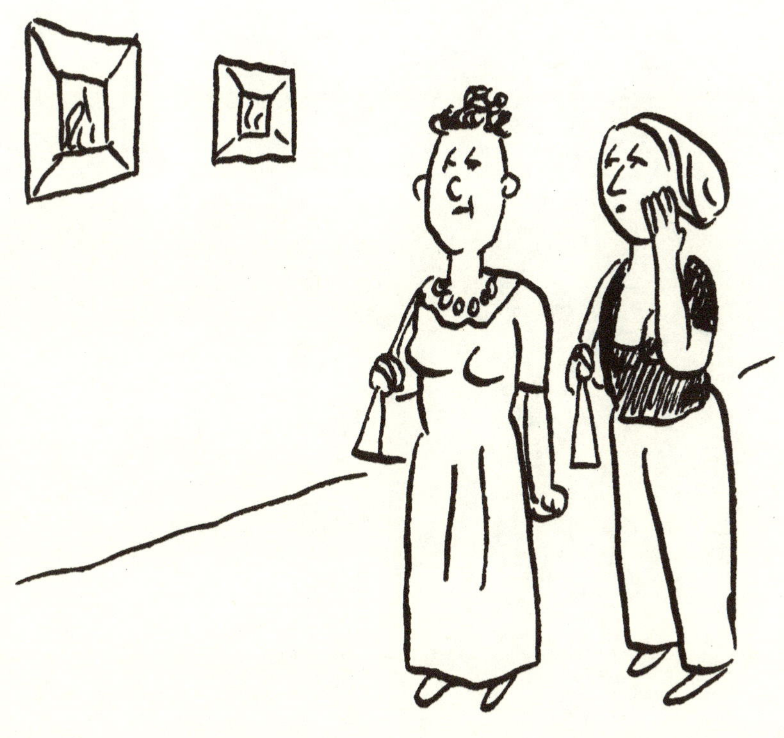

"He obviously didn't read the last issue of October."

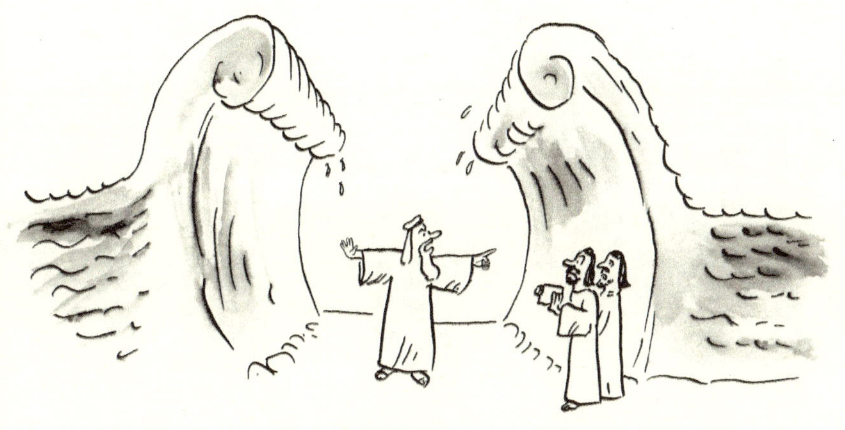

"Please, no documentation! This is an ephemeral work."

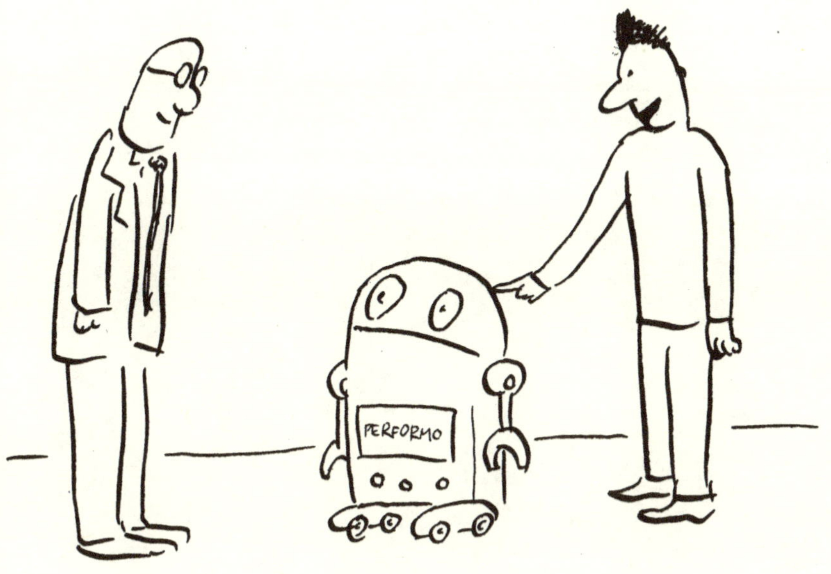

"And then when you put it on Seventies Mode it does Acconci reenactments."

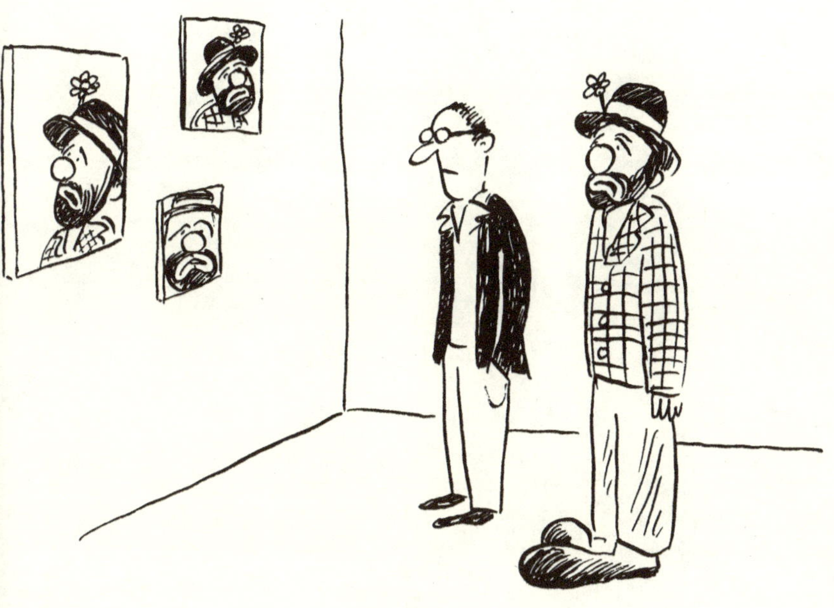

"Yes, but Bruce Nauman wasn't sincere like me."

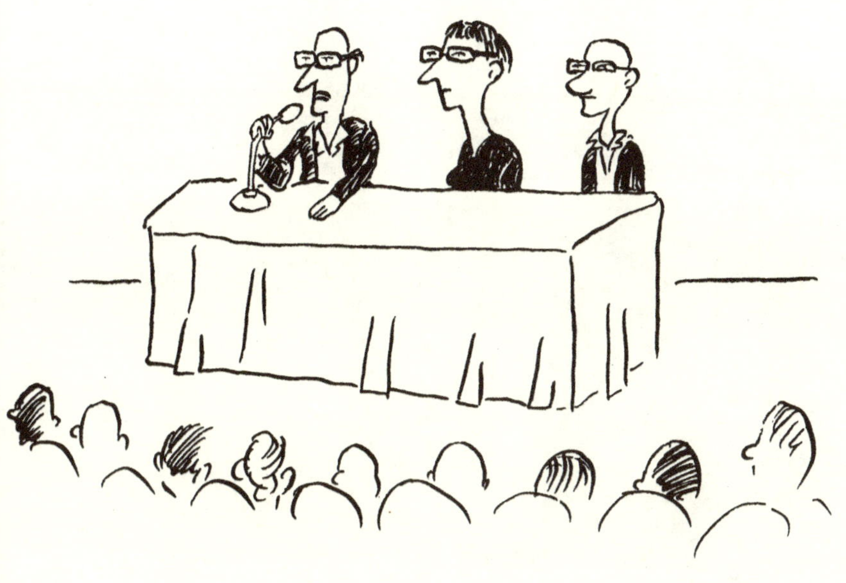

"And I guess now we will just sit here and try to show some interest while you ask us stupid questions."

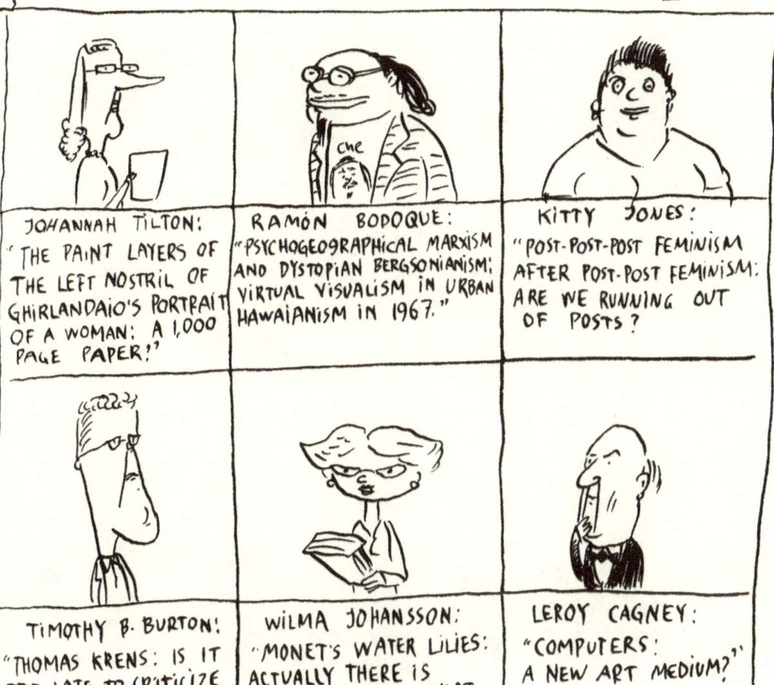
Most memorable
ART CONFERENCE PAPERS
JOHANNAH TILTON:
"THE PAINT LAYERS OF THE LEFT NOSTRIL OF GHIRLANDAIO'S PORTRAIT OF A WOMAN: A 1,000 PAGE PAPER!"
CHE
RAMÓN BODOQUE:
"PSYCHOGEOGRAPHICAL MARXISM AND DYSTOPIAN BERGSONIANISM: VIRTUAL VISUALISM IN URBAN HAWAIIANISM IN 1967."
KITTY JONES:
"POST-POST-POST FEMINISM AFTER POST-POST FEMINISM: ARE WE RUNNING OUT OF POSTS?
TIMOTHY B. BURTON:
"THOMAS KRENS: IS IT TOO LATE TO CRITICIZE HIM NOW?"
WILMA JOHANSSON:
"MONET'S WATER LILIES: ACTUALLY THERE IS SOMETHING MORE THAT CAN BE SAID ABOUT THEM"
LEROY CAGNEY:
"COMPUTERS: A NEW ART MEDIUM?"

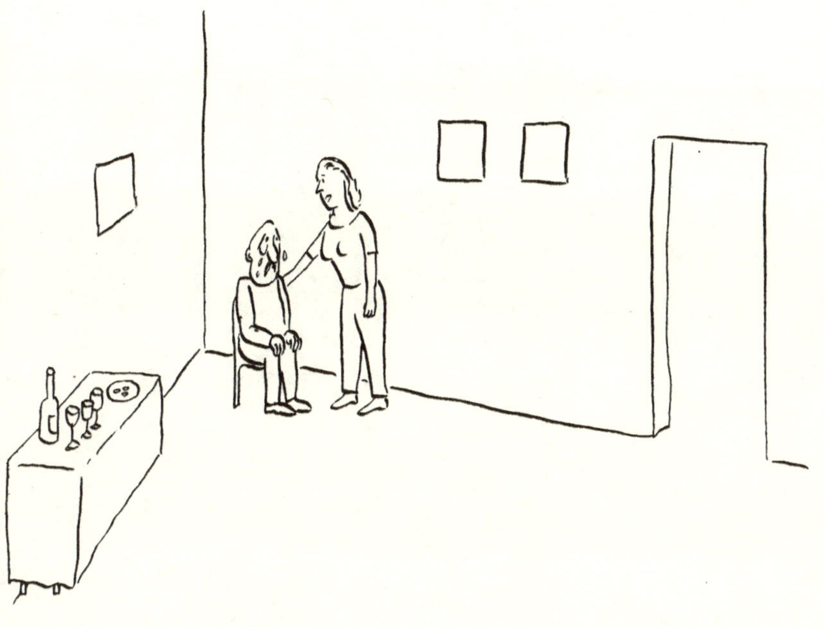

"But look at the upside: no one will ever know that nobody ever came to your opening."

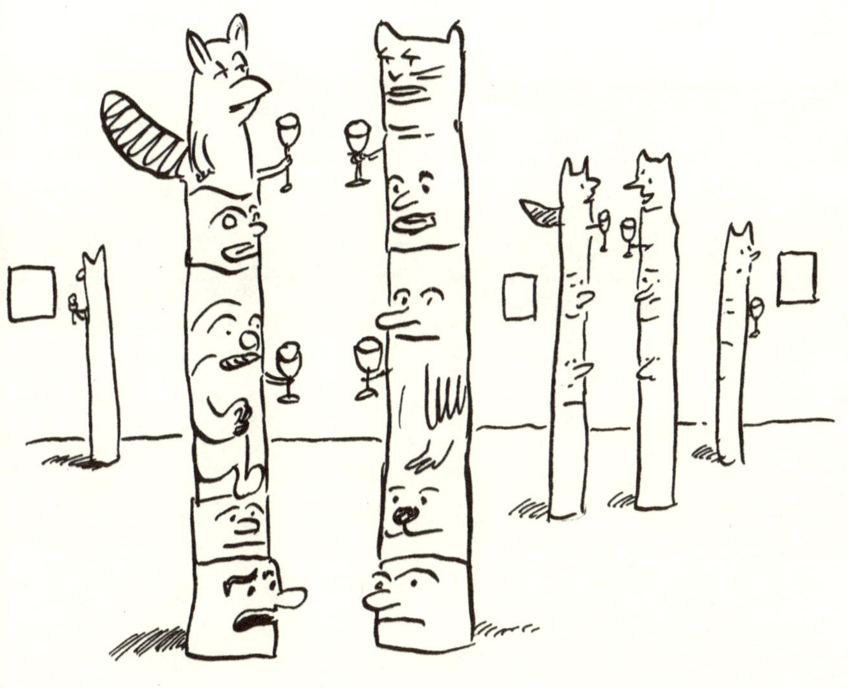

"Don't you hate these openings where you are at the bottom of the totem pole?"

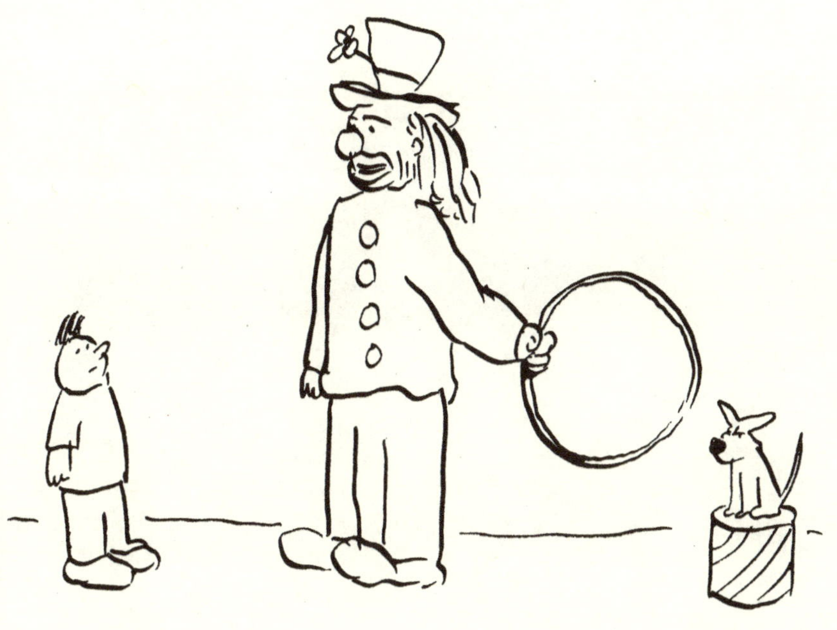

"When I was your age, I was a Young British Artist."

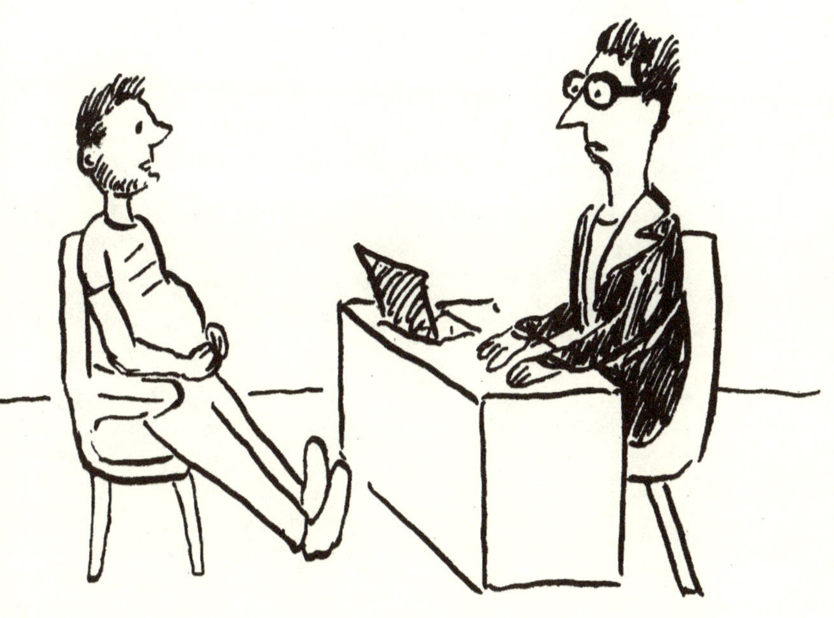

"If I agree for you to represent my work, will the gallery ensure to update my Wiki entry every week?"

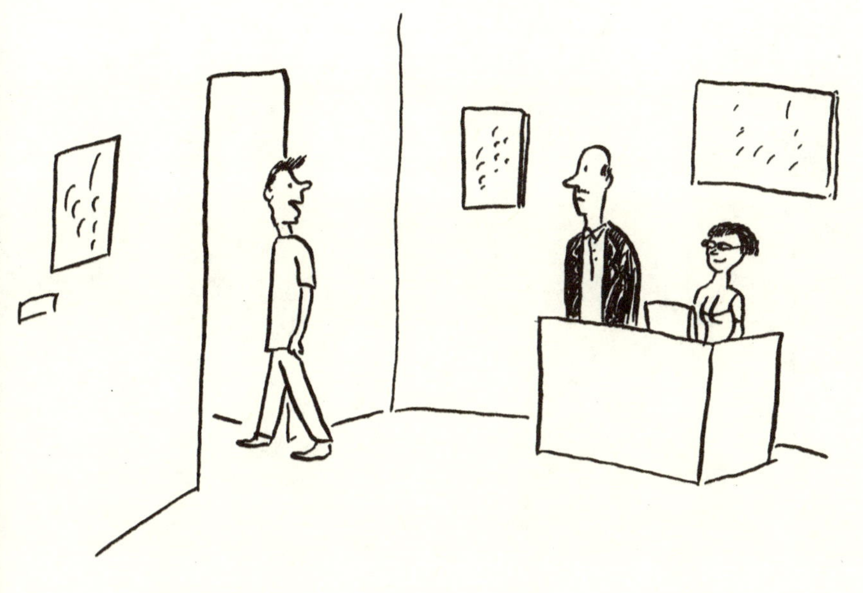

"Your shows suck, but your gallerina totally rocks."

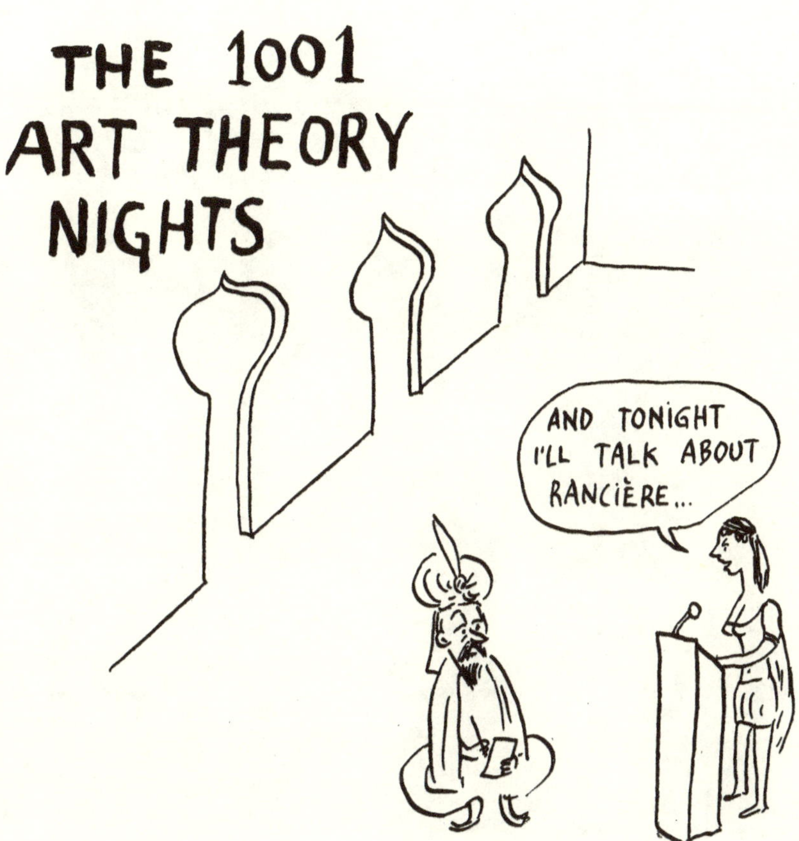
THE 1001
ART THEORY
NIGHTS
AND TONIGHT
I'LL TALK ABOUT
RANCIÈRE...

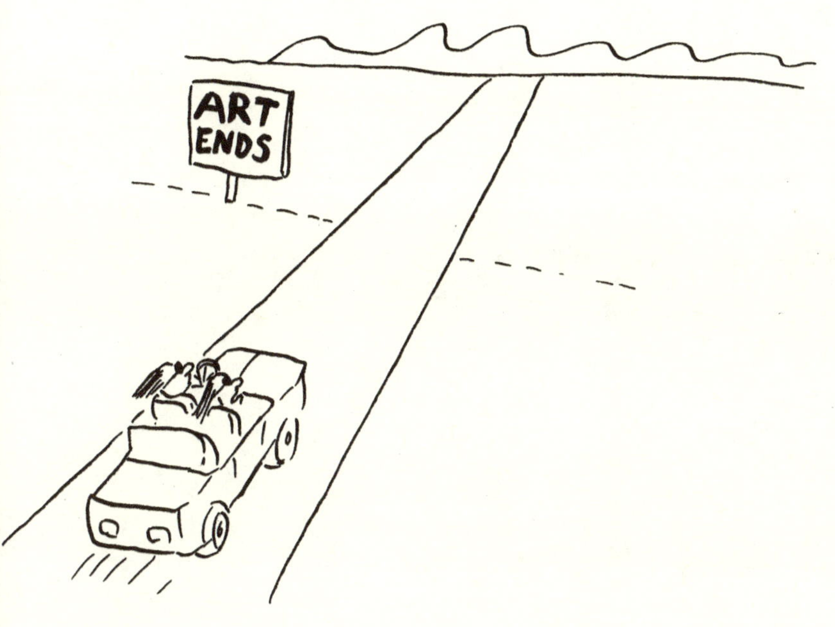

"Are we in Design now?"

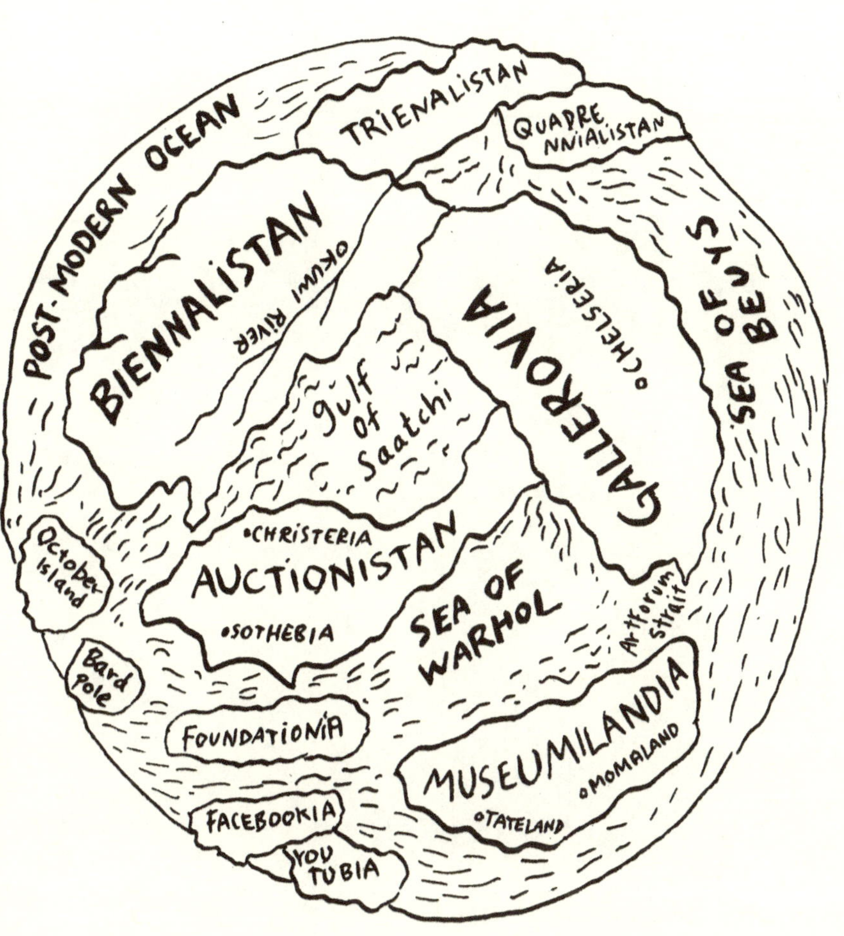
POST-MODERN OCEAN
TRIENALISTAN
QUADRE NNIALISTAN
BIENNALISTAN
OKUWI RIVER
GALLEROVIA
CHELSERIA
SEA OF BEUYS
Gulf of Saatchi
CHRISTERIA
AUCTIONISTAN
SOTHEBIA
October Island
SEA OF WARHOL
Artforum strait
Bard Pole
FOUNDATIONIA
MUSEUMILANDIA
MOMALAND
TATELAND
FACEBOOKIA
YOU TUBIA

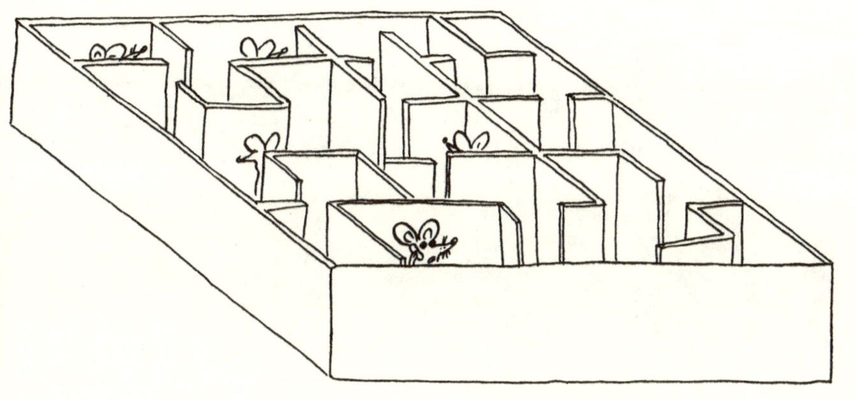

"I am at some weird Swedish gallery.
Did you find the cheese?"

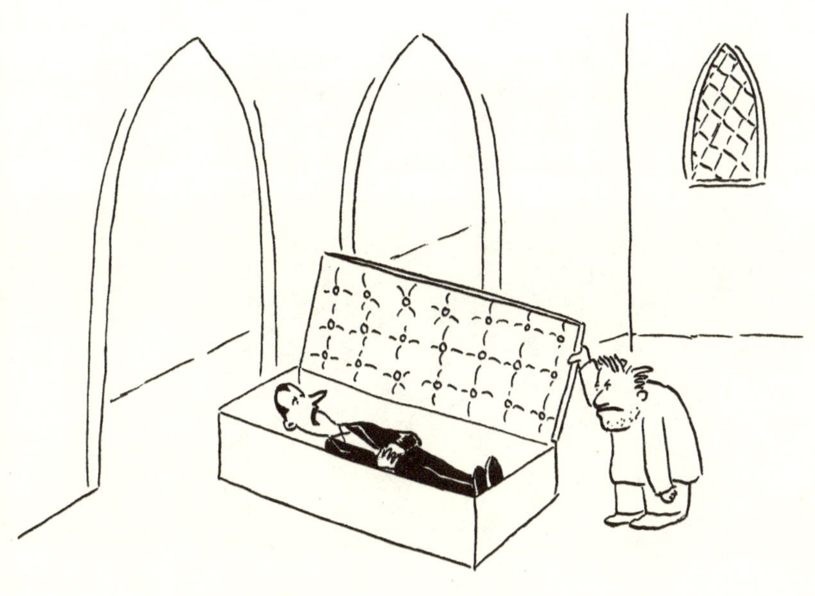

"Just wake me up for the next Documenta."

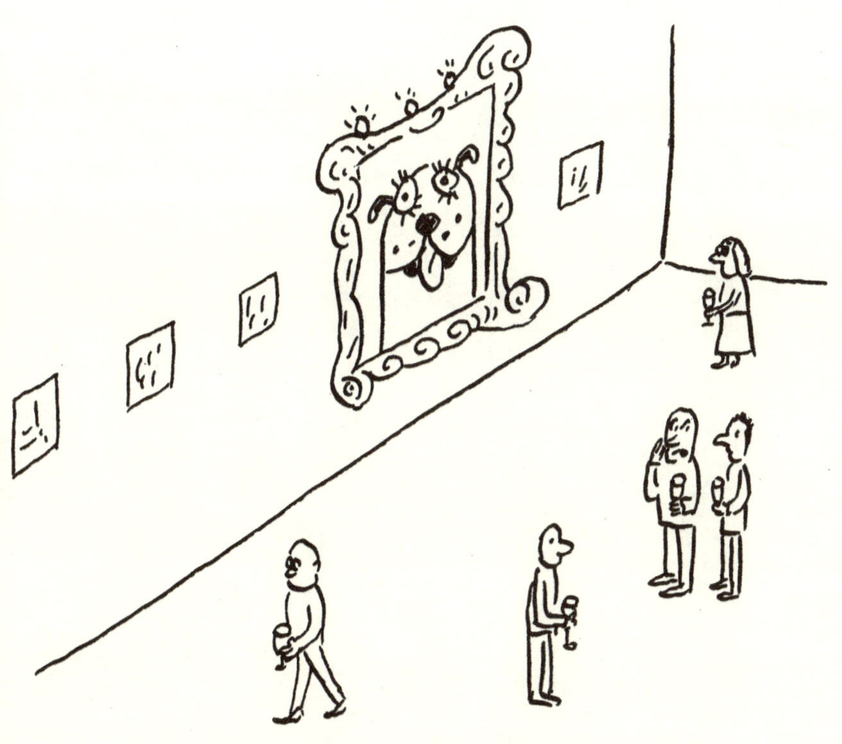

"I had to include the painting of the funder's girlfriend, but no one can tell."

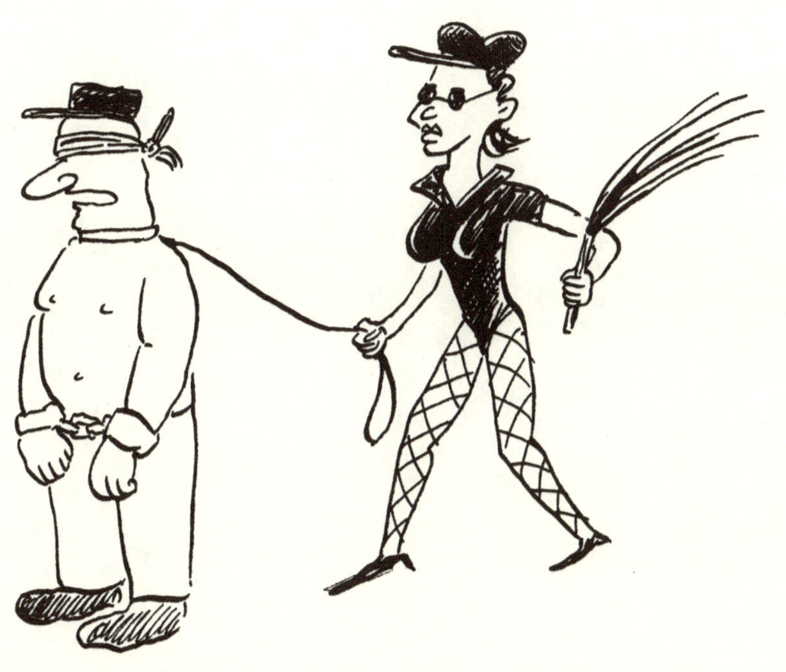

"I want to be your found object."

# of ARTFAIRS PAST

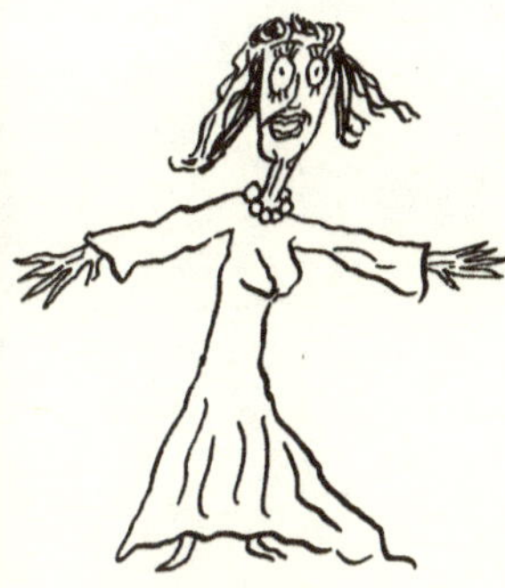

THE CRAZY COLLECTOR WHO NEVER PAYS

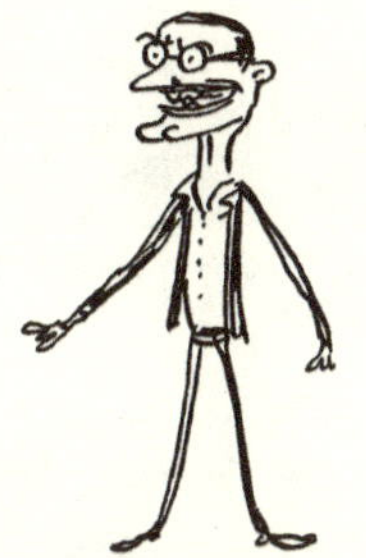

THE TRAITOR ARTIST WHO SWITCHED GALLERIES

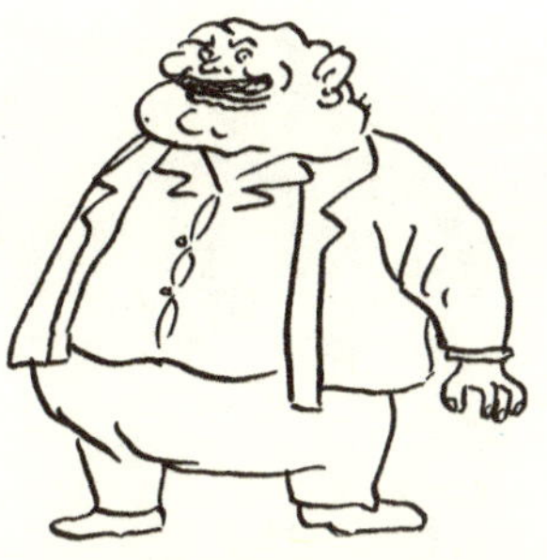

THE SLIMY DEALER WHO PREYS ON ART STUDENTS

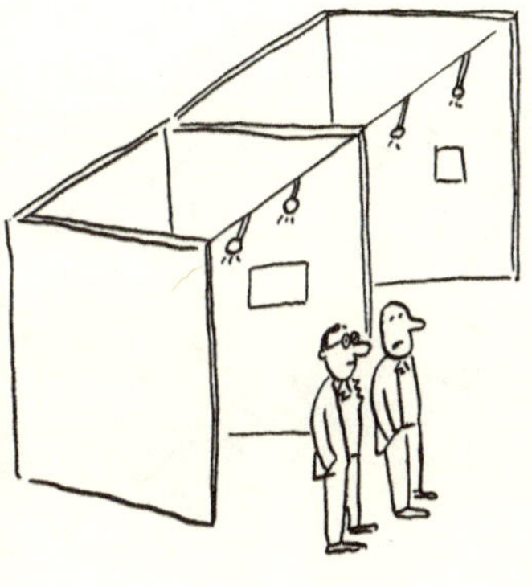

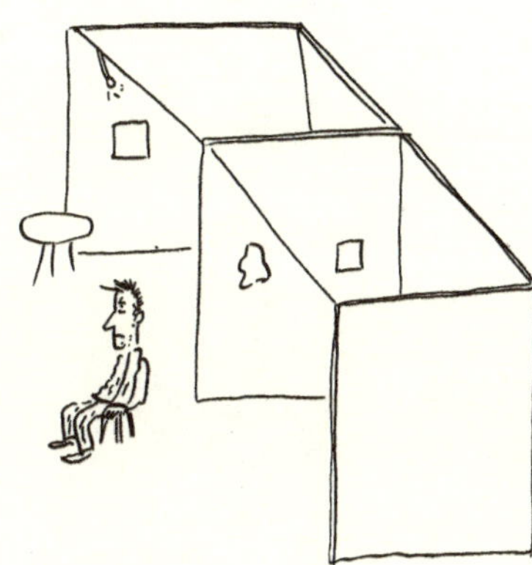

"He hasn't had the time to go home and change between artfairs."

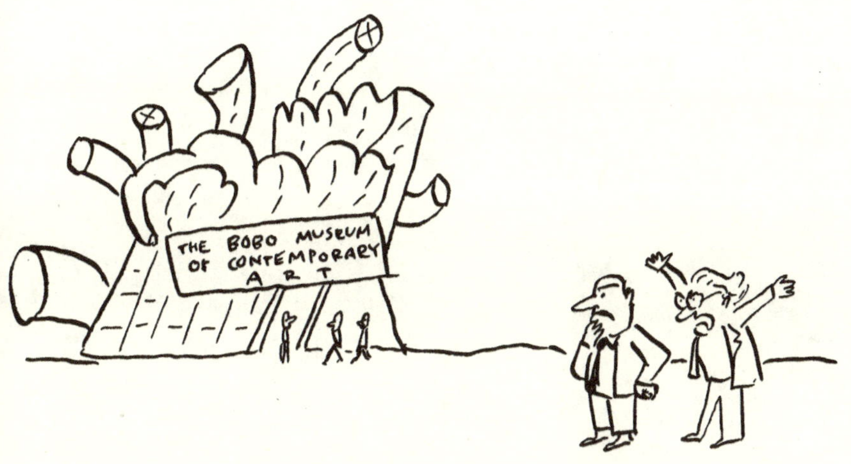

"OK, I designed a distracting building, but that's because it is supposed to show bad art."

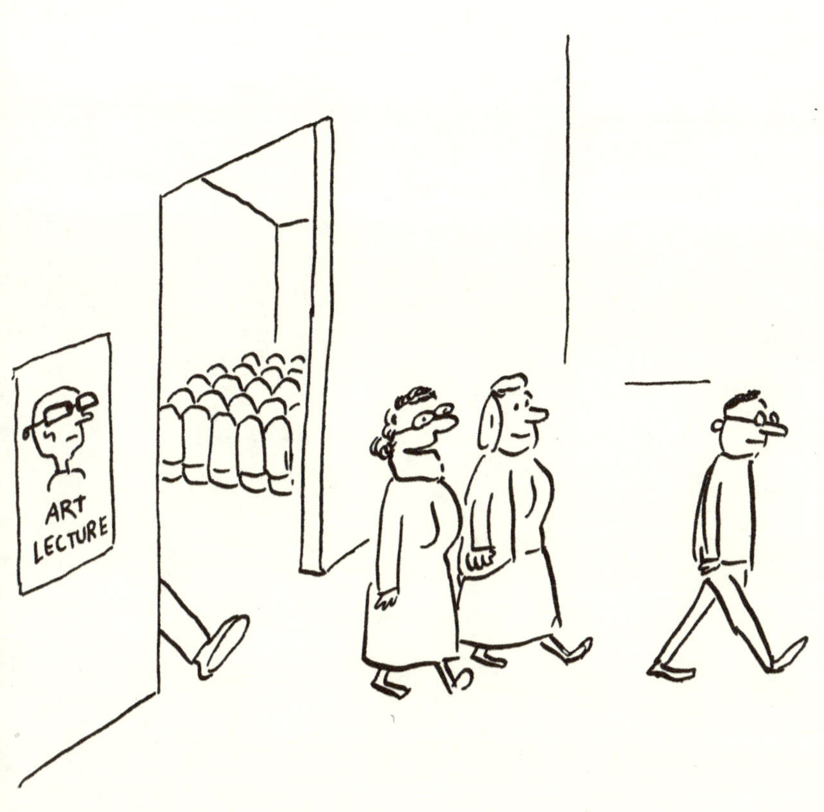

"I didn't understand anything, but he felt brilliant."

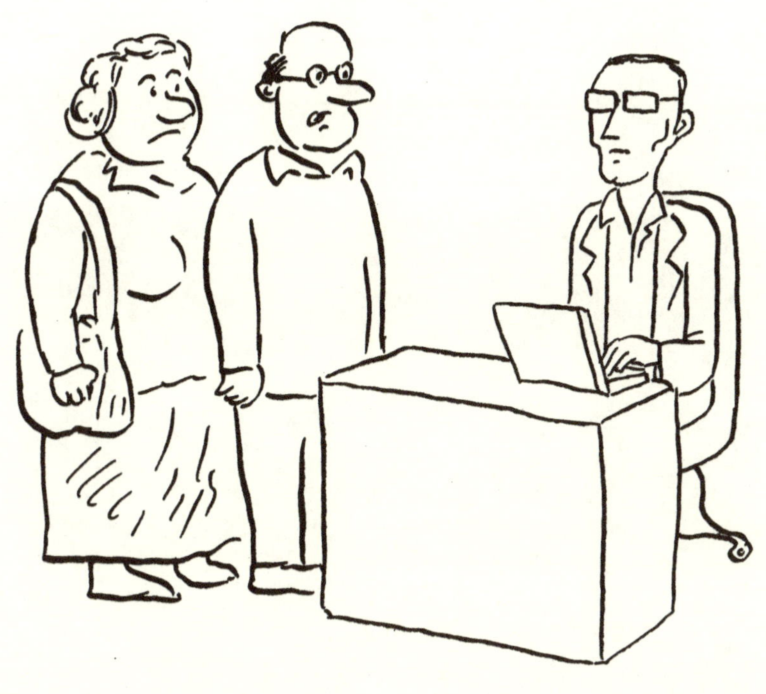

"I don't think it's a Duane Hanson—
it's just the gallery assistant."

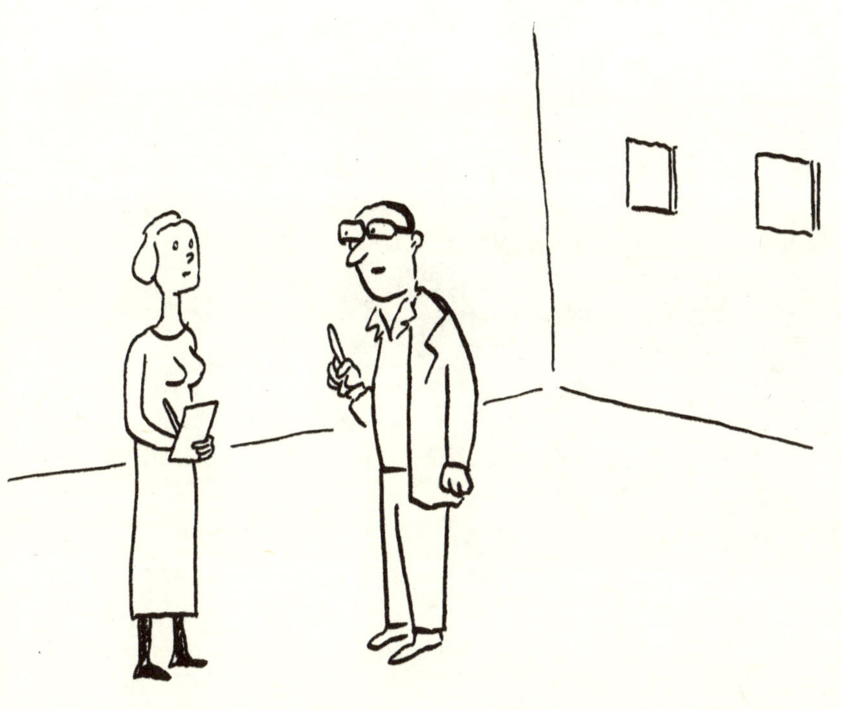

"If he doesn't blink when you say the price, then quickly add, 'unframed.' "

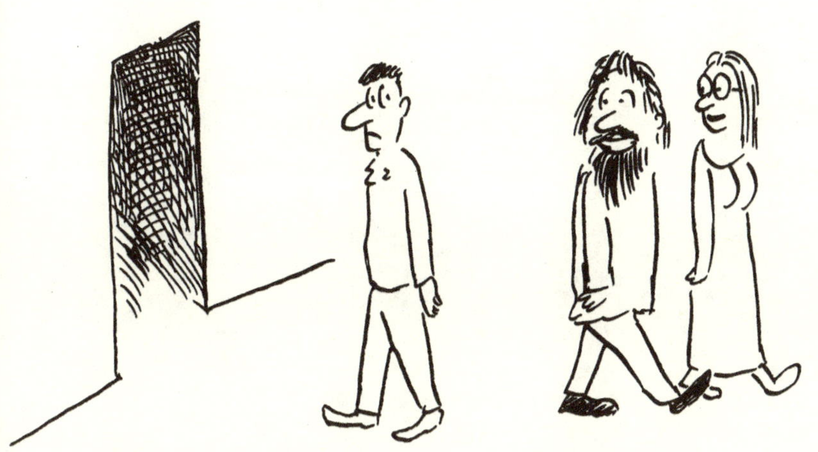

"It's a long video. We started watching it in 1979."

artfacebook

Status updates

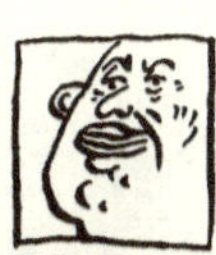

Barry is casually rubbing in your face that he got a famous collector to buy his work.

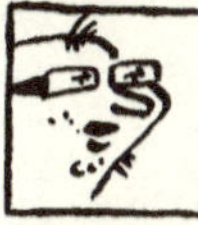

Randy won't talk to you in person at openings but he will be your **FB** friend.

Lina says she is insanely busy at the studio but has enough time to change her status updates every hour.

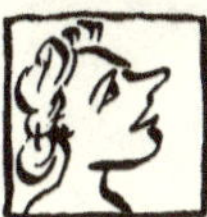

Britanny put a 15 year-old profile picture of herself and thinks no one will notice.

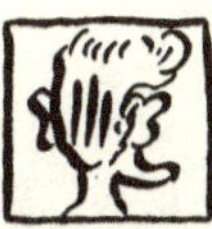

Matthew forwards you teddy bears and still thinks you will take him seriously as an artist.

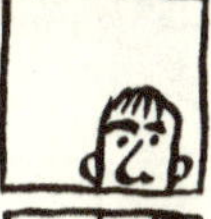

Barry says he is in Leipzig installing in some weird-sounding art space no one has heard of.

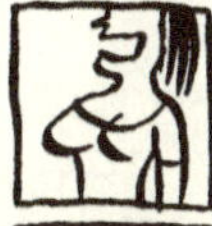

Shahana is in Venice, but you have no idea why she is in your **FB** list.

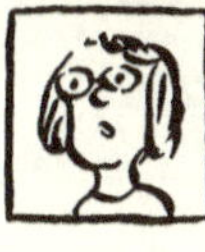

Mary Ann is an important curator trying to be cool by joining **FB.**

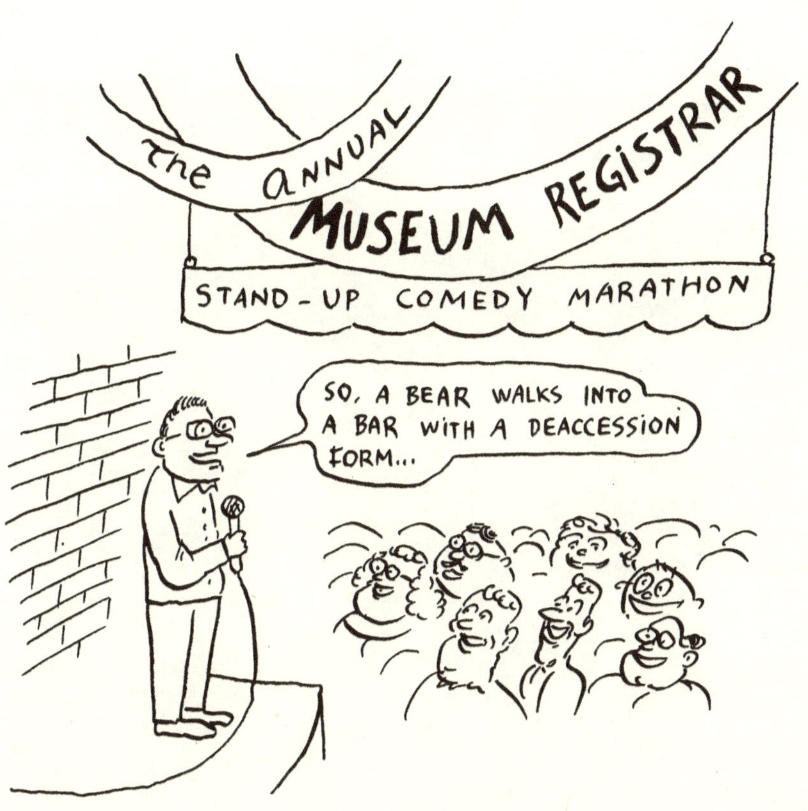
the annual
MUSEUM REGISTRAR
STAND-UP COMEDY MARATHON
SO, A BEAR WALKS INTO A BAR WITH A DEACCESSION FORM...

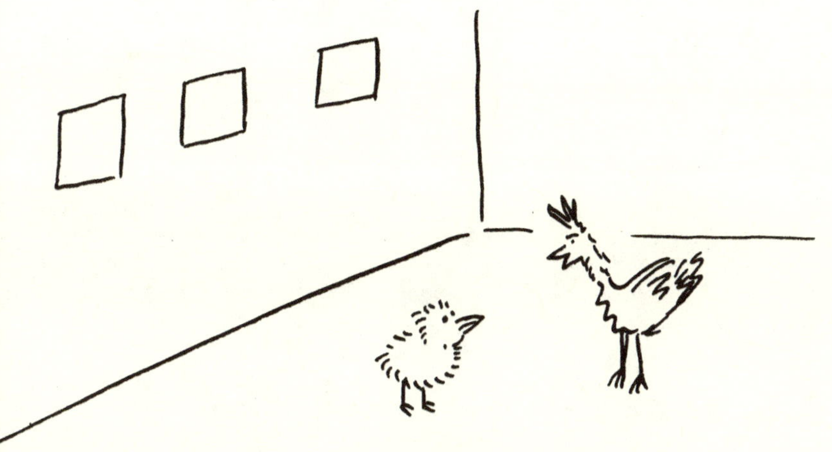

"Now you are a cute chick, but wait until you become mid-career."

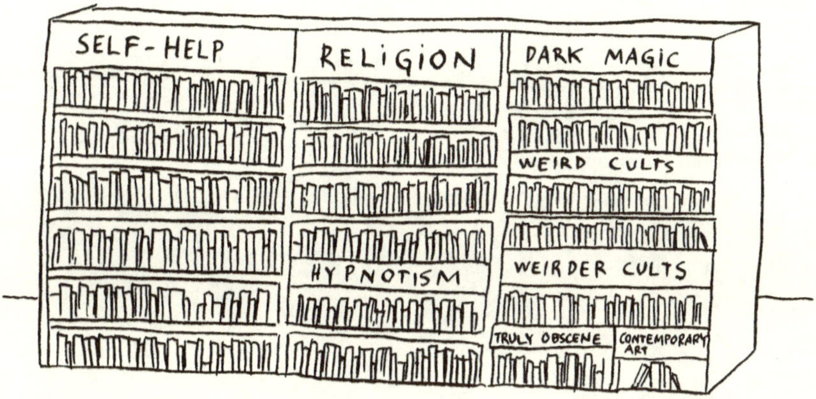

SELF-HELP
RELIGION
DARK MAGIC
WEIRD CULTS
HYPNOTISM
WEIRDER CULTS
TRULY OBSCENE
CONTEMPORARY ART

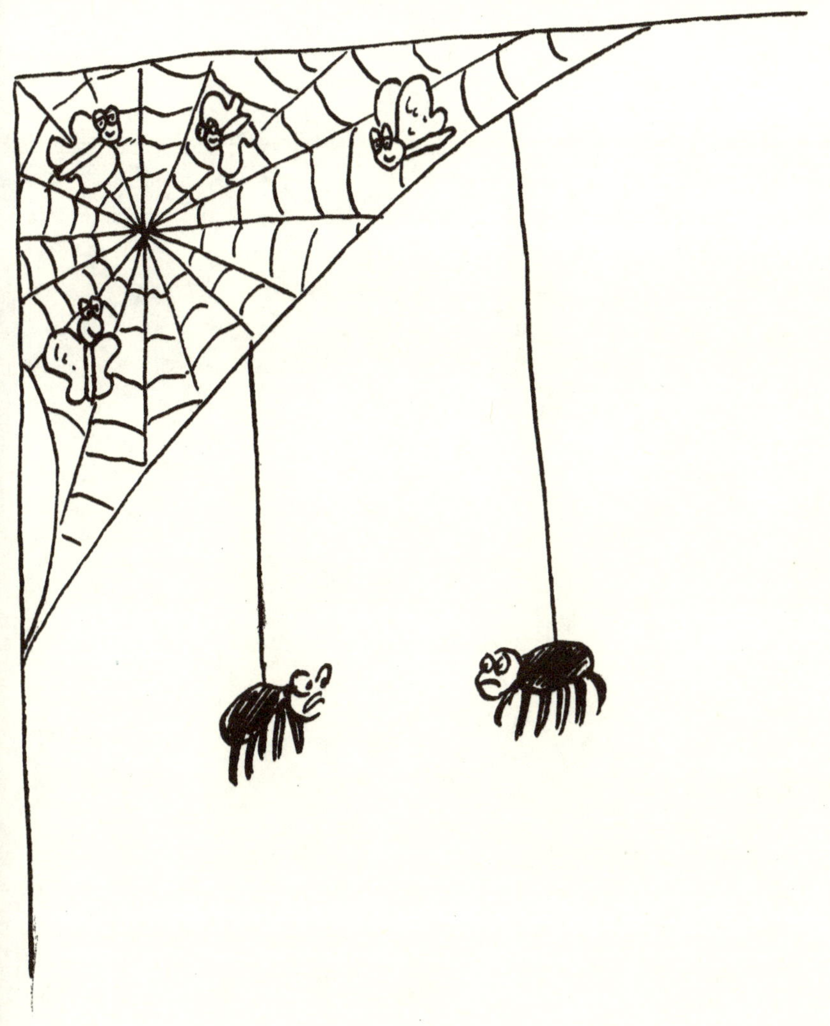

"I keep trying to attract buyers, but instead I keep getting stuck with all these social butterflies."

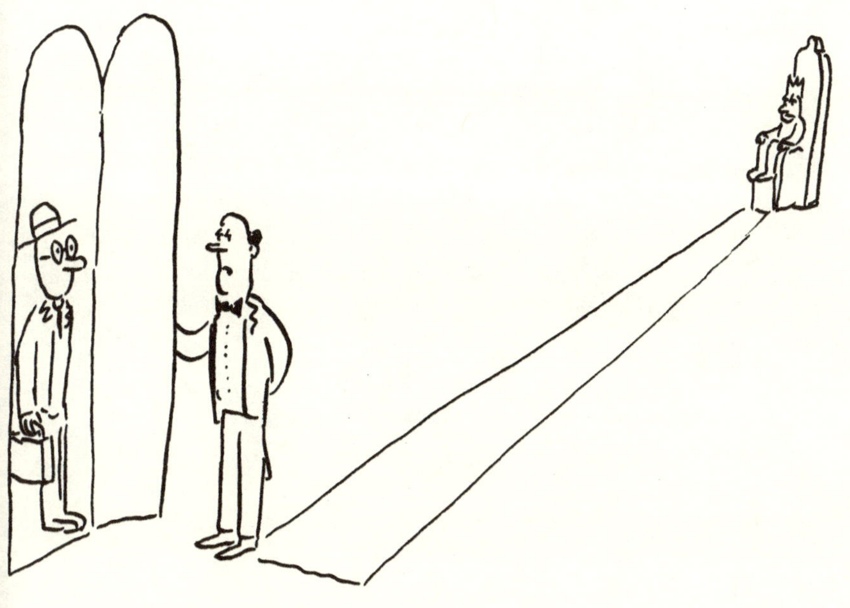

"The blue-chip artist will see you now."

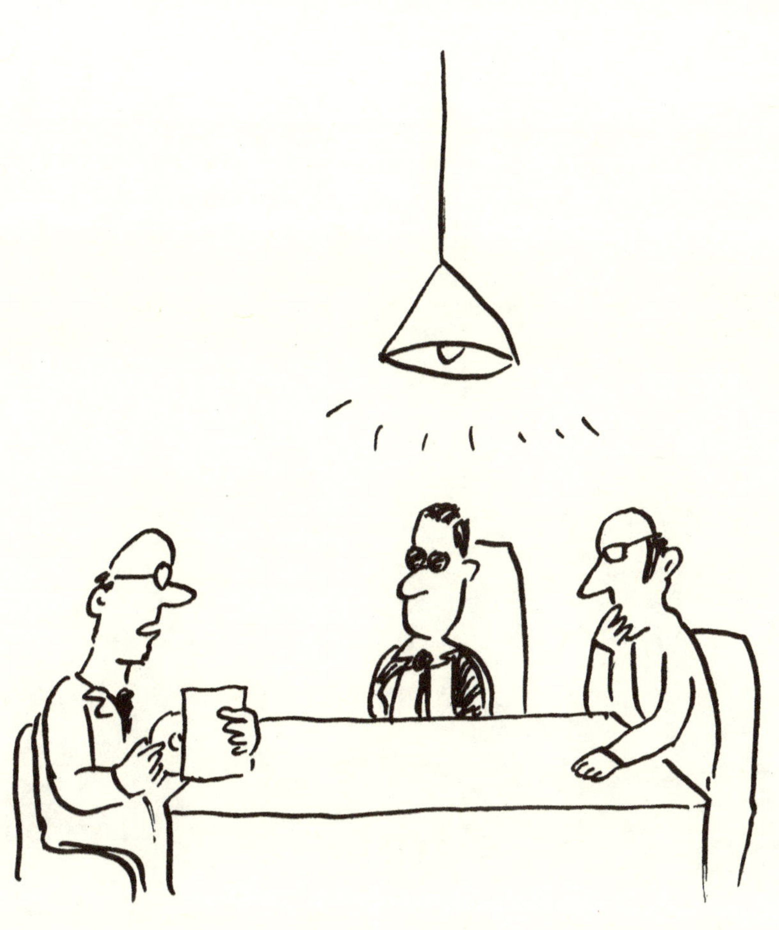

"This time Al-Qaeda mailed a three-channel video, edition of five."

yet UNREALIZED CHRISTO & JEANNE-CLAUDE PROJECTS

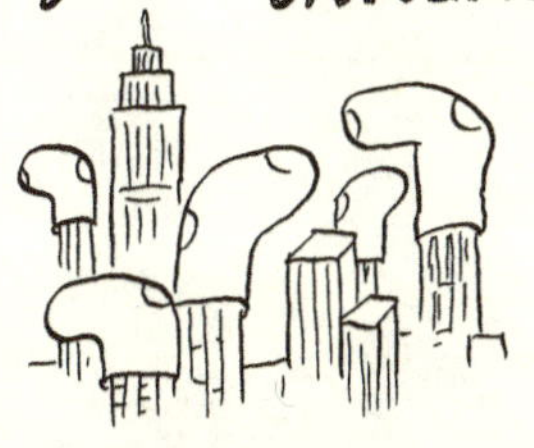

THE SOCKS

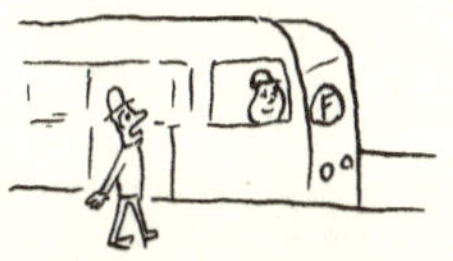

THE NYC SUBWAY RUNNING ON SATURDAYS

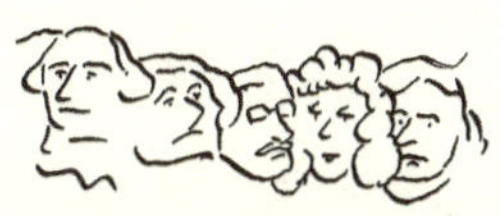

JEANNE-CLAUDE'S FACE ON MOUNT RUSHMORE

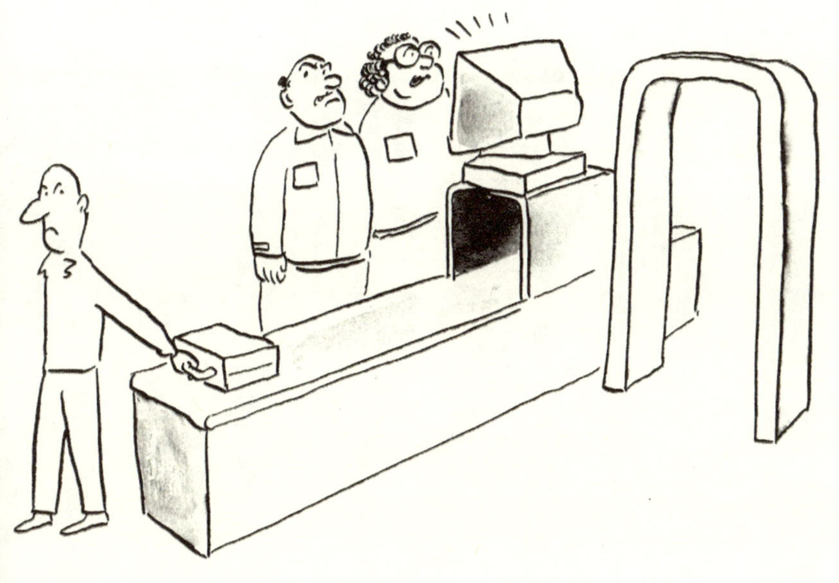

"Was that Richard Serra's Tilted Arch?"

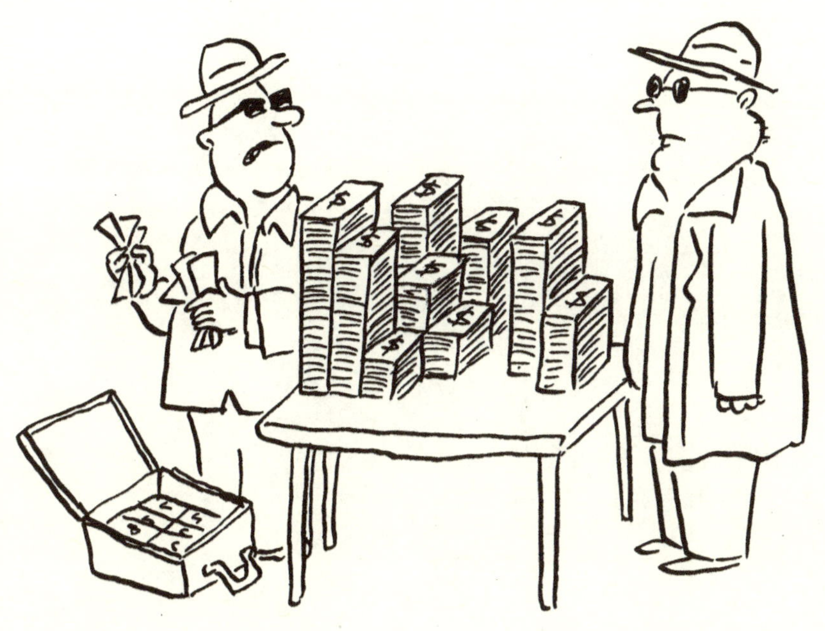

"What do you mean a casino?
An auction house is a better front."

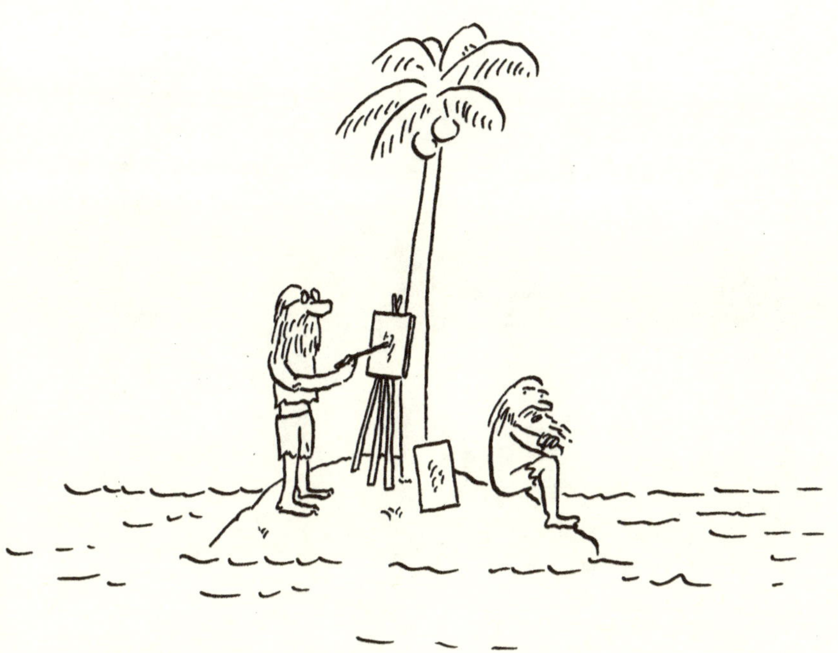

"You are overflooding the market."

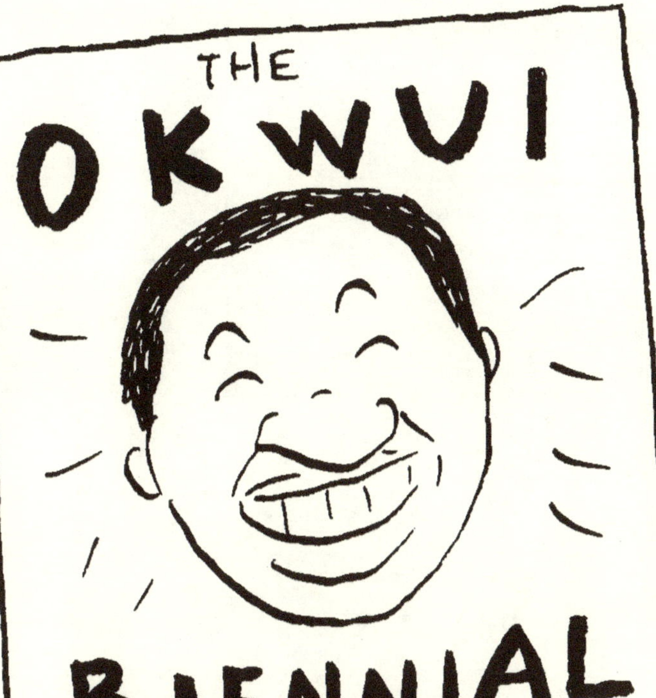
THE
OKWUI
BIENNIAL
CURATED, DIRECTED,
AND ENTIRELY STARRED
BY OKWUI
NOW IN TRZWAMBUL
PRODUCED BY OKWUI, ...OKWUI
OKWUI THIS OKWUI THAT
& OH YES, THERE ARE ARTISTS IN IT

THE SOUTH CHELSEA OPENINGS DIET

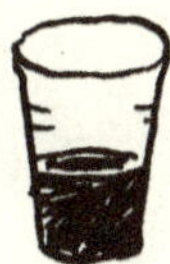

IDAHO
CABERNET,
0.15¢ BOTTLE

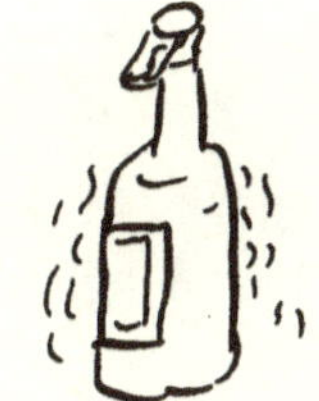

HOT
BEER

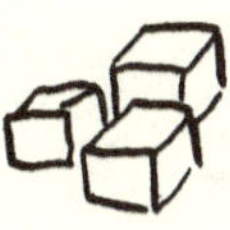

FLUORESCENT
MONTEREY
JACK
MINIMALIST
CHEESE
CUBES

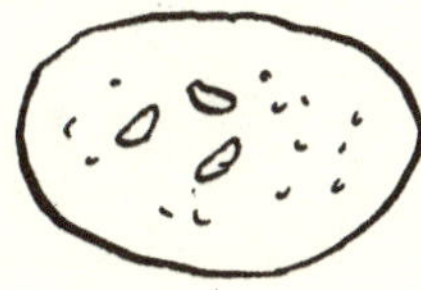

THREE
GREASY
PEANUTS

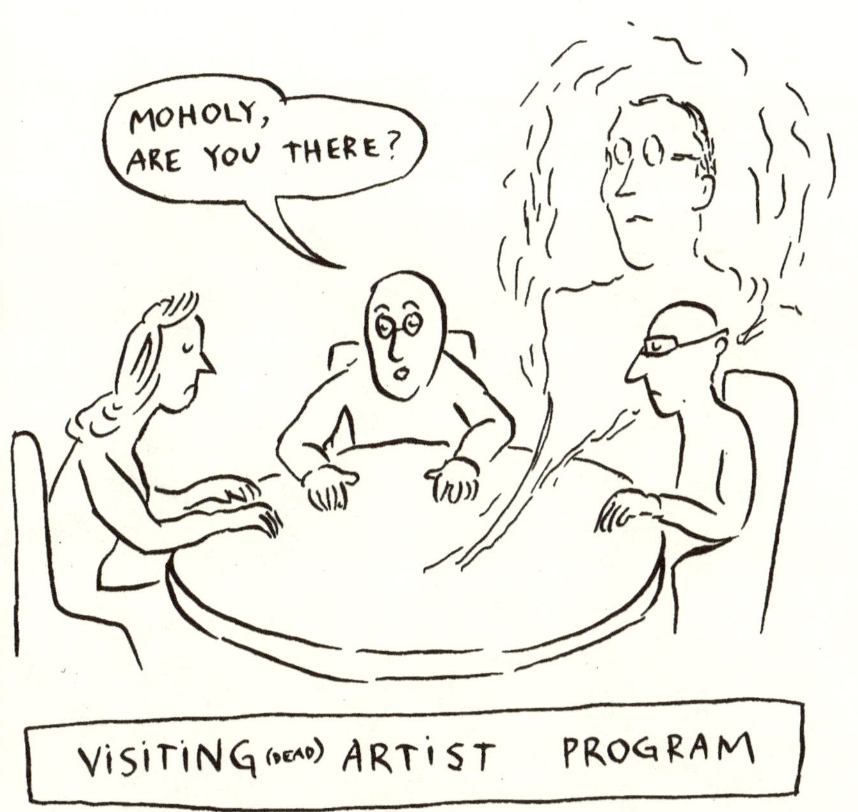
MOHOLY, ARE YOU THERE?
VISITING (DEAD) ARTIST PROGRAM

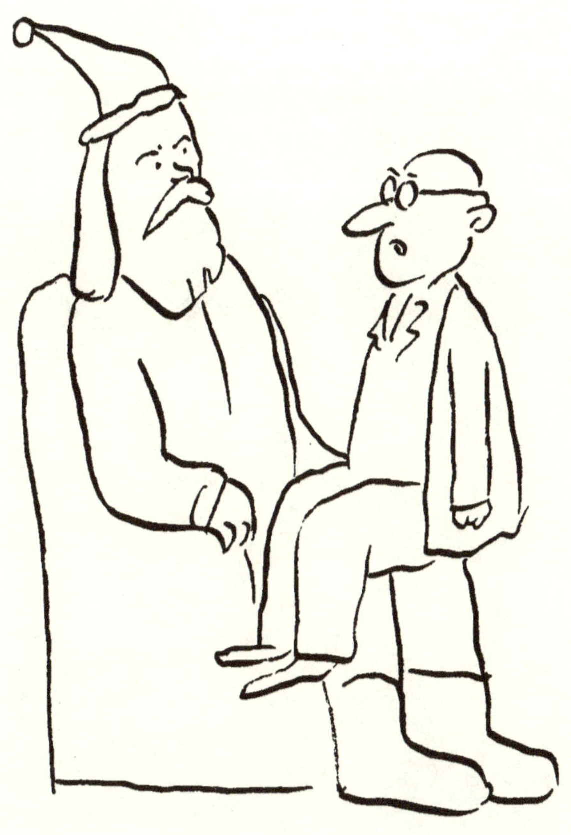

"I want exclusivity."

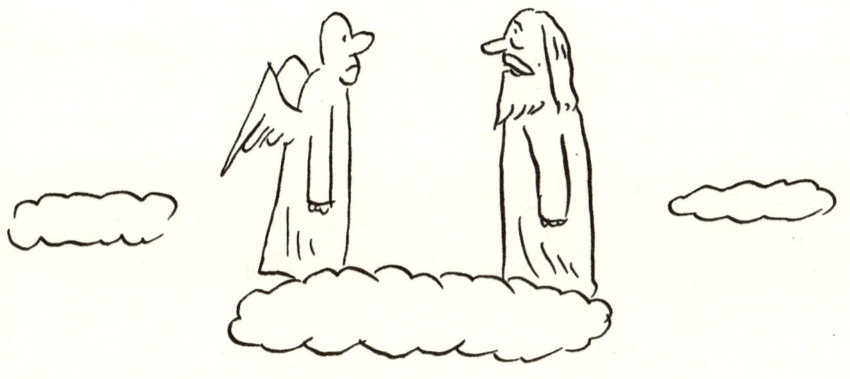

"I know it's cool to be God. I just would prefer to be Mathew Barney."

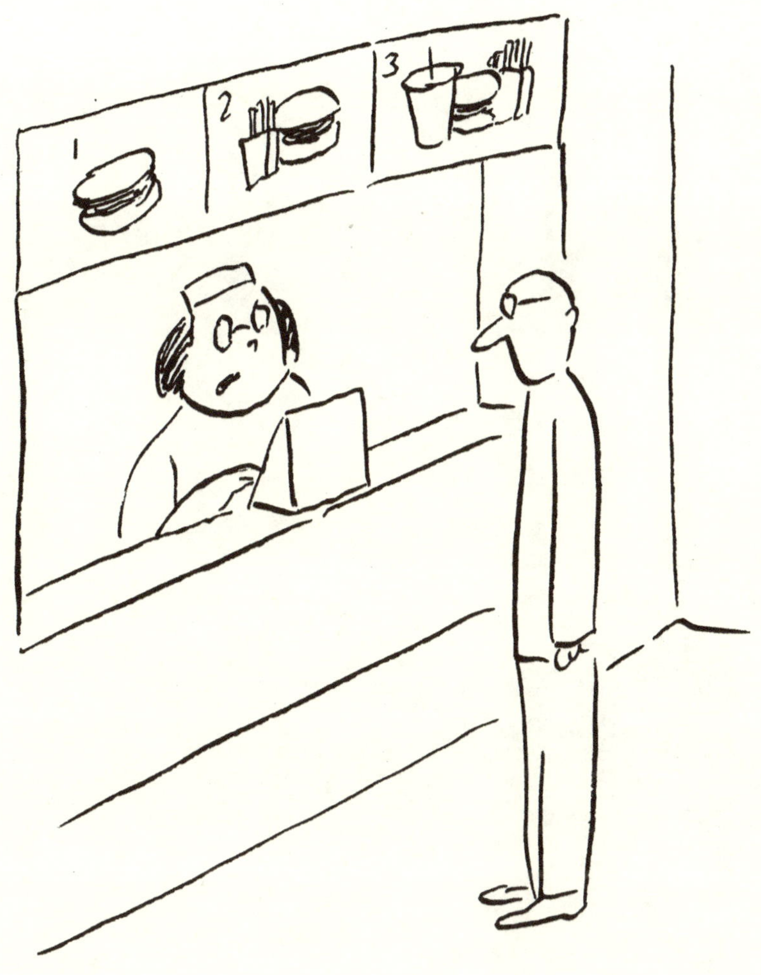

"Do you want to biennale-size it?"

Pablo Helguera is a visual artist. Some of his past art projects have included making a phonographic archive of dying languages, creating scripted symposia performed by actors (unbeknownst to the audience), building a memory theater, and founding a research institute exploring the global impact of Latin American soap operas. He is the author of five books, including *The Pablo Helguera Manual of Contemporary Art Style* (2007) and the novel *The Boy Inside the Letter* (2008), published by Jorge Pinto Books.

In 2006 he drove from Anchorage to Tierra del Fuego with a collapsible schoolhouse, organizing discussions and civic ceremonies (The School of Panamerican Unrest). In 2008 he received a Guggenheim Fellowship.

He lives in Brooklyn with his wife Dannielle Tedeger and their cat ceniza.

András Szántó, a writer and researcher on cultural affairs, is a senior lecturer at the Sotheby's Institute of Art in New York and co-founder of artworldsalon.com.

www.ingramcontent.com/pod-product-compliance
Lightning Source LLC
LaVergne TN
LVHW090958080826
845145LV00003B/1045

* 9 7 8 1 9 3 4 9 7 8 1 0 8 *